For more than 50 years, *The Australian Women's Weekly* Test Kitchen has been creating marvellous recipes that come with a guarantee of success. First, the recipes always work — just follow the instructions and you too will get the results you see in the photographs. Second, and perhaps more importantly, they are delicious — created by experienced home economists and chefs, all triple-tested and, thanks to their straightforward instructions, easy to make.

In *Alice's Adventures in Wonderland*, Lewis Carroll said it all, perfectly...

"Beautiful soup, so rich and green, waiting in a hot tureen!

Who for such dainties would not stoop?

Soup of the evening, beautiful soup! Beautiful soup!

Who cares for fish, Game, or any other dish?

Who would not give all else for two Pennyworth only of beautiful soup?"

My feelings exactly — and I know they'll be yours, too, once you start cooking from this book. One of the oldest-known prepared foods, one that is seemingly infinite in its possibilities, one that is restorative, comforting and (perhaps above all else) absolutely delicious — soup, beautiful soup. Enjoy.

Pamela Clark

FOOD EDITOR

contents

stock up on the basics

These recipes can be made up to 2 days ahead and stored, covered, in the refrigerator.
Be sure to remove and discard any solidified fat from the surface of the cooled stock.
If the cooled stock is to be kept longer than that, freeze it in quantities appropriate
to your needs. These recipes make about 2.5 litres (10 cups) of stock.

BEEF STOCK

2kg meaty beef bones
2 medium brown onions (300g)
2 trimmed celery sticks (150g),
  chopped coarsely
2 medium carrots (250g),
  chopped coarsely
3 bay leaves
2 teaspoons black peppercorns
5 litres water (20 cups)
3 litres water (12 cups), extra

Place bones and unpeeled coarsely
chopped onions in baking dish.
Roast, uncovered, in hot oven for
about 1 hour or until bones and
onions are well browned. Transfer
bones and onions to large
saucepan; add celery, carrot, bay
leaves, peppercorns and the water.
Simmer, uncovered, for 3 hours,
skimming surface occasionally.
Add the extra water; simmer,
uncovered, for 1 hour, skimming
surface occasionally. Strain stock
mixture through muslin-lined
strainer into large clean bowl.

FISH STOCK

1.5kg fish bones
3 litres water (12 cups)
1 medium onion (150g), chopped
2 trimmed celery sticks (150g),
  chopped coarsely
2 bay leaves
1 teaspoon black peppercorns

Combine ingredients in large
saucepan. Simmer, uncovered,
20 minutes; strain as in Beef Stock.

1 Roast bones and onions in hot oven
until well browned.

2 Skim froth from the surface of the
simmering stock.

CHICKEN STOCK

2kg chicken bones
2 medium brown onions (300g),
  chopped coarsely
2 trimmed celery sticks (150g),
  chopped coarsely
2 medium carrots (250g),
  chopped coarsely
3 bay leaves
2 teaspoons black peppercorns
5 litres water (20 cups)

Combine ingredients in large
saucepan. Simmer, uncovered,
2 hours; strain as in Beef Stock.

VEGETABLE STOCK

2 large carrots (360g),
  chopped coarsely
2 large parsnips (360g),
  chopped coarsely
4 medium brown onions (600g),
  chopped coarsely
12 trimmed celery sticks (900g),
  chopped coarsely
4 bay leaves
2 teaspoons black peppercorns
6 litres water (24 cups)

Combine ingredients in large
saucepan. Simmer, uncovered,
1 1/2 hours; strain as in Beef Stock.

3 *Strain the stock through fine muslin to remove solids.*

traditional

Grandma's noodle soup is equally loved whether translated into Japanese somen broth, Malaysian laksa or Chinese hot and sour soup – of all the courses of a meal, none provides us with such appetising proof of the existence of a culinary melting pot than does the universally loved soup.

potage st germain

PREPARATION TIME 10 MINUTES (plus soaking time) • COOKING TIME 1 HOUR 15 MINUTES

This classic pea soup from France is known throughout the world. Another variation is called potage puree de pois a la menthe, *which is basically this soup flavoured with the addition of a great deal of shredded fresh mint. The French have three words for soup:* consommé, *a thin broth;* soupe, *a traditional thick soup with discernible pieces of meat, vegetables, etc; and* potage, *soup which is processed until smooth and thickened with cream or eggs.*

Adding split peas to the water

2 cups green split peas (400g)
1 litre water (4 cups)
1 tablespoon olive oil
1 large brown onion (200g), chopped coarsely
1 clove garlic, crushed
2 trimmed sticks celery (150g), chopped coarsely
1.25 litres chicken stock (5 cups)
500g frozen peas

1 Soak split peas in the water in a large bowl for 3 hours or overnight.

2 Heat oil in large saucepan; cook onion and garlic, stirring, until onion is soft. Stir in celery; cook, stirring, 2 minutes.

3 Add undrained peas and stock, bring to a boil; simmer, uncovered, about 1 hour or until peas are tender (skimming the surface and stirring occasionally). Stir in frozen peas; cook, stirring, about 10 minutes or until peas are tender.

4 Blend or process soup, in batches, until pureed; push through food mill or large sieve into large clean saucepan. *[Can be made ahead to this stage. Cover; refrigerate overnight or freeze.]*

5 Just before serving, stir over heat until soup is hot.

SERVES 6

per serve 5.2g fat; 1354kJ

serving suggestion Sprinkle with chopped fresh mint and add a dollop of crème fraîche to serve.

tip Add 300ml of cream when processing the soup for a richer, smoother variation.

indonesian meatball soup

PREPARATION TIME 20 MINUTES • COOKING TIME 2 HOURS 15 MINUTES

This is a variation on the renowned bakso of eastern Java that's sold by street hawkers and in bakso restaurants which serve nothing but! Make it and you'll soon see why it's so popular. Many versions contain thin wheat noodles; you can cook 250g of your favourite noodles in this soup just before serving.

2kg chicken bones (carcass, neck, wings, etc)
2 medium brown onions (300g), chopped coarsely
2 trimmed celery sticks (150g), chopped coarsely
2 medium carrots (250g), chopped coarsely
4 litres water (16 cups)
1 small white onion (80g), chopped finely
2 cloves garlic, crushed
500g veal mince
2 tablespoons ketjap manis
2 tablespoons soy sauce
1 cup bean sprouts (80g)
4 green onions, sliced thinly

1 Combine bones, brown onion, celery, carrot and the water in large saucepan; bring to a boil. Simmer, uncovered, 2 hours; strain through muslin-lined strainer into large bowl. Reserve stock; discard bones and vegetables. *[Can be made ahead to this stage. Cover; refrigerate overnight or freeze.]*

2 Using hands, combine white onion, garlic, veal, half of the ketjap manis and half of the soy sauce in large bowl; roll rounded teaspoons of veal mixture into balls. Place on tray, cover; refrigerate 30 minutes. *[Can be made ahead to this stage. Cover; refrigerate overnight or freeze.]*

3 Combine remainder of both sauces with stock in large saucepan; bring to a boil. Add meatballs; simmer, uncovered, stirring occasionally, about 10 minutes or until meatballs are cooked through.

4 Divide soup among serving bowls; top with bean sprouts and green onion.

SERVES 6

per serve 2.1g fat; 1016kJ

serving suggestion Accompany this soup with separate bowls of steamed jasmine rice and stir-fried Asian greens.

tips Cook meatballs in soup close to serving time, to prevent soup from becoming cloudy.

• Use commercially made stock if you don't want to make your own.

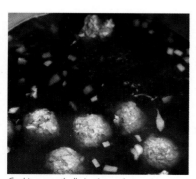

Cooking meatballs in simmering soup

zuppa di risoni

This Italian pasta and vegetable soup is not dissimilar to the one your grandmother used to make. Risoni, a small rice-shaped pasta, can be substituted with orzo or pastina if you prefer.

4 litres water (16 cups)
3 large carrots (540g),
    chopped coarsely
2 large brown onions (400g),
    chopped coarsely
4 trimmed sticks celery (300g),
    chopped coarsely
1 tablespoon black peppercorns
4 bay leaves
10 sprigs fresh flat-leaf parsley
1 tablespoon olive oil
1 large brown onion (200g),
    chopped coarsely, extra
2 cloves garlic, crushed
150g pancetta, chopped coarsely
2 medium carrots (240g),
    chopped coarsely, extra
2 medium potatoes (400g),
    chopped coarsely
2 sprigs fresh rosemary
1 cup risoni (220g)
1/4 cup loosely packed,
    coarsely chopped fresh
    flat-leaf parsley, extra

1 Combine the water, carrot, onion, celery, peppercorns, bay leaves and parsley in large saucepan; bring to a boil. Simmer, uncovered, 1 1/2 hours; strain over large bowl. Reserve stock; discard vegetables. *[Can be made ahead to this stage. Cover; refrigerate overnight or freeze.]*

2 Heat oil in large saucepan; cook extra onion, garlic and pancetta, stirring, until onion is soft. Add extra carrot, potato and rosemary; cook, stirring, 5 minutes. Stir in stock, bring to a boil; simmer, uncovered, about 10 minutes or until vegetables are tender.

3 Stir in pasta, bring to a boil; simmer, uncovered, about 5 minutes or until risoni is just tender. Stir extra parsley into soup.

SERVES 6

per serve 7.2g fat; 1114kJ
serving suggestion This soup makes a meal when accompanied by an antipasti platter and fresh ciabatta.

Adding risoni to soup

wonton soup

PREPARATION TIME 30 MINUTES • COOKING TIME 40 MINUTES

This Chinese favourite is also known as short soup. Wonton wrappers, packaged small square pastry sheets, are available from many supermarkets and any Asian food outlet.

**2 teaspoons peanut oil
2 cloves garlic, crushed
2 litres chicken stock (8 cups)
1 tablespoon soy sauce
1 litre water (4 cups)
4 green onions, sliced thinly**

WONTONS

**1 tablespoon peanut oil
4 green onions, sliced thinly
2 cloves garlic, crushed
1 tablespoon grated ginger
400g minced pork
2 tablespoons soy sauce
36 wonton wrappers
1 egg, beaten lightly**

1 Heat oil in large saucepan; cook garlic, stirring, 2 minutes. Stir in stock, soy sauce and the water, bring to a boil; simmer, uncovered, 15 minutes. *[Can be made ahead to this stage. Cover; refrigerate overnight or freeze.]*

2 Just before serving, divide wontons among serving bowls; pour over hot soup, sprinkle with onion.

wontons Heat oil in large frying pan; cook onion, garlic, and ginger, stirring, until onion is soft. Add pork; cook, stirring, until pork is just browned, stir in soy sauce. Place rounded teaspoons of cooled pork mixture in centre of each wrapper; brush edges with egg, pinch edges together to seal. Repeat with remaining wrappers, pork mixture and egg.

SERVES 6

per serve 16.6g fat; 1980kJ
serving suggestion Serve as an entree to a Chinese meal.
tips Gow gee wrappers can be substituted for wonton wrappers.
• Wrap unused wonton wrappers in plastic and freeze up to 2 months.

STEP I   STEP 2   STEP 3   STEP 4

Making wontons
Place I rounded teaspoon of filling on each wonton wrapper.
Brush around edges of wrappers with lightly beaten egg.
Gather the 4 edges of wrappers together around the filling.
Pinch the edges of wrappers together to form a pouch shape.

harira

PREPARATION TIME 20 MINUTES (plus soaking time)
COOKING TIME 2 HOURS 10 MINUTES

This hearty lamb and vegetable soup from Morocco is traditionally eaten during the four weeks of Ramadan, after sundown, to break the day's fast.

1/2 cup dried chickpeas (100g)
500g boned shoulder of lamb
2 tablespoons olive oil
1 large brown onion (200g),
  chopped coarsely
2 teaspoons ground ginger
1 tablespoon ground cumin
1 teaspoon ground cinnamon
2 teaspoons ground coriander
6 saffron threads
3 trimmed celery sticks (225g),
  chopped coarsely
7 medium tomatoes (1.3kg),
  seeded, chopped coarsely
2.5 litres water (10 cups)
1/2 cup brown lentils (100g)
1/4 cup loosely packed, coarsely
  chopped fresh coriander leaves

1 Place chickpeas in small bowl, cover with water; soak overnight, drain.

2 Trim lamb of excess fat; cut into 2cm cubes.

3 Heat oil in large saucepan; cook onion, stirring, until soft. Add spices; cook, stirring, about 2 minutes or until fragrant. Add lamb and celery; cook, stirring, about 2 minutes or until lamb is coated in spice mixture. Add tomato; cook, stirring, about 10 minutes or until tomato slightly softens. Stir in the water and drained chickpeas; bring to a boil. Simmer, covered, about 1 1/2 hours or until lamb is tender, stirring occasionally.

4 Stir in lentils; cook, covered, about 30 minutes or until lentils are just tender. *[Can be made ahead to this stage. Cover; refrigerate overnight.]*

5 Just before serving, stir fresh coriander into soup.

SERVES 6

per serve 15.6g fat; 1317kJ

serving suggestion Serve with lemon wedges and toasted pide.

tips Drained canned chickpeas can be substituted for dried chickpeas.

• Two 400g cans of tomatoes can be substituted for fresh tomatoes.

Cutting the trimmed lamb into cubes

Adding lentils to the simmering soup

stracciatella

PREPARATION TIME 5 MINUTES • COOKING TIME 10 MINUTES

Stracciatella, *when translated from Italian to English, means strings or torn rags. This satisfying soup is thus aptly named, since this is what the parmesan and egg mixture resembles once it meets the hot stock.*

5 eggs
1/2 cup finely grated parmesan cheese (40g)
1.5 litres chicken stock (6 cups)
2 tablespoons finely chopped fresh flat-leaf parsley
pinch nutmeg

1   Lightly whisk eggs with cheese in medium jug until combined.

2   Bring stock to a boil in large saucepan. Remove from heat; gradually add egg mixture, whisking constantly.

3   Return mixture to heat; simmer, stirring constantly, about 5 minutes or until egg mixture forms fine shreds. Stir in parsley and nutmeg.

SERVES 6

per serve   6.9g fat; 606kJ

serving suggestion   Serve as perfect "comfort" food – accompanied only by a loaf of ciabatta.

tips   Break the eggs one at a time into a small cup before adding together in the bowl; this way, if one egg is stale, you can discard it.

•   Make sure you add the egg and cheese mixture gradually or you will end up with large clumps of "scrambled" egg.

Finely grating the parmesan cheese

Whisking egg-and-cheese mixture into stock

bouillabaisse

PREPARATION TIME 35 MINUTES • COOKING TIME 45 MINUTES

Born on the Mediterranean coast around Marseilles, this classic French dish was originally made by local fisherman with what was unsold of their daily catch. A main-dish seafood soup, bouillabaisse is always made using local fish, thus explaining the immense changes in overall colour and flavour among the many regional variations. Rouille, a red sauce made with capsicums and chillies, and aioli, that intense garlic mayonnaise, traditionally accompany bouillabaisse wherever it is served.

500g mussels
1kg scampi
2 tablespoons olive oil
**2 small leeks (400g),
    chopped finely**
**1 large fennel bulb (650g),
    sliced thinly**
2 cloves garlic, crushed
**1 red Dutch chilli, seeded,
    chopped finely**
**6 medium tomatoes (1.2kg),
    peeled, chopped coarsely**
2 litres fish stock (8 cups)
6 saffron threads
**400g firm white fish fillets,
    chopped coarsely**
200g scallops
**2 tablespoons coarsely chopped
    fresh flat-leaf parsley**

AIOLI

4 cloves garlic, quartered
2 egg yolks
2 tablespoons lemon juice
1 cup olive oil (250ml)

ROUILLE

2 medium red capsicums (400g)
**2 red Thai chillies, seeded,
    chopped coarsely**
1 clove garlic, quartered
2 tablespoons stale breadcrumbs
1/4 cup olive oil (60ml)

1 Scrub mussels under cold water; remove beards. Shell and devein half of the scampi; remove heads from remaining half.

2 Heat oil in large heavy-base saucepan; cook leek, fennel, garlic and chilli, stirring, about 10 minutes or until leek softens. Add tomato, stock and saffron; bring to a boil. Simmer, uncovered, about 20 minutes or until tomato is pulpy, stirring occasionally. Strain mixture into large clean saucepan; discard vegetables. *[Can be made ahead to this stage. Cover; refrigerate overnight.]*

3 Bring stock mixture to a boil. Add mussels and scampi; simmer, covered, about 10 minutes or until all mussels open (discard any that do not).

4 Add fish and scallops to pan; simmer, uncovered, 5 minutes. Just before serving, stir in parsley. Serve with aioli and rouille.

aioli Blend or process garlic, egg yolks and juice until creamy. With motor operating, gradually add oil; process until aioli thickens. *[Can be made ahead. Cover; refrigerate overnight.]*

rouille Quarter capsicums, remove and discard seeds and membranes. Roast under grill or in very hot oven, skin-side up, until skin blisters and blackens. Cover capsicum pieces in plastic or paper for 5 minutes; peel away skin, chop coarsely. Process capsicum, chilli, garlic and breadcrumbs until combined. With motor operating, gradually add oil; process until rouille thickens. *[Can be made ahead. Cover; refrigerate overnight.]*

SERVES 6

per serve 61g fat; 3191kJ
serving suggestion Serve with a fresh crisp baguette.

tip Use your favourite seafood in this recipe: squid, prawns or crab are tasty substitutions, and any sort of fish fillets can be used.

Peeling tomatoes

Deveining scampi

pumpkin soup

PREPARATION TIME 20 MINUTES • COOKING TIME 35 MINUTES

Any type of pumpkin can be used for this soup, however, we prefer to use butternut pumpkin because of its sweet flavour, sparse seed content and comparatively thin skin.

Adding pumpkin and potato to pan

40g butter
1 large brown onion (200g), chopped coarsely
1.5kg pumpkin, chopped coarsely
2 large potatoes (600g), chopped coarsely
1.5 litres chicken stock (6 cups)
1/2 cup cream (125ml)

1 Melt butter in large saucepan; cook onion, stirring, until soft. Stir in pumpkin and potato; cook, stirring, 5 minutes.

2 Stir in stock, bring to a boil; simmer, uncovered, about 20 minutes or until pumpkin is soft, stirring occasionally.

3 Blend or process soup, in batches, until pureed; push through food mill or large sieve into large clean saucepan. *[Can be made ahead to this stage. Cover; refrigerate overnight or freeze.]*

4 Just before serving, add cream; stir over heat until soup is hot. Serve topped with a dollop of sour cream and a few chives, if desired.

SERVES 6

per serve 14.8g fat; 1346kJ

serving suggestion This soup is great as the first course of a roast chicken dinner.

tip Pushing the soup through a food mill or a sieve after the initial blending or processing results in an almost velvet-smooth texture.

minestrone

PREPARATION TIME 25 MINUTES (plus soaking time) • COOKING TIME 1 HOUR 10 MINUTES

There are almost as many versions of minestrone as there are Italian families, but this recipe is a typical example of those made in the north, where the colder winters require hearty fare like this. Ditalini or ditali are small hollow pasta tubes; tiny macaroni can be substituted.

**1/2 cup dried cannellini
   beans (100g)**
2 teaspoons olive oil
**1 medium brown onion (150g),
   chopped finely**
2 cloves garlic, crushed
**10 slices prosciutto (150g),
   chopped coarsely**
**1 trimmed celery stick (75g),
   chopped finely**
**1 medium carrot (120g),
   chopped finely**
**1 medium green zucchini (120g),
   chopped finely**
2 x 400g cans tomatoes
1.5 litres chicken stock (6 cups)
**1 medium potato (200g),
   chopped finely**
1 cup ditalini (170g)
**1 cup loosely packed finely
   shredded savoy cabbage (80g)**
**1 cup loosely packed, finely
   shredded spinach leaves**
**1 tablespoon finely shredded
   fresh basil leaves**
**1/2 cup finely grated parmesan
   cheese (40g)**

1 Place beans in medium bowl, cover with water; stand overnight, drain.

2 Heat oil in large saucepan; cook onion and garlic, stirring, until onion is soft. Add prosciutto, celery, carrot and zucchini; cook, stirring, 5 minutes. Stir in undrained crushed tomatoes and stock. Bring to a boil; simmer, uncovered, 30 minutes. *[Can be made ahead to this stage. Cover; refrigerate overnight or freeze.]*

3 Stir in beans and potato; simmer, uncovered, 15 minutes.

4 Add pasta; simmer, uncovered, about 10 minutes or until pasta is tender.

5 Just before serving, stir in cabbage, spinach and basil; serve soup with a separate bowl of the cheese.

SERVES 6

per serve 8.7g fat; 1472kJ

serving suggestions Serve as a main course with Italian bread and mixed green salad.

tips Make the basic soup mixture (up to and including step 2) when you soak the beans (ie, the day before required), to allow the flavours to develop.

• Leftover steamed and chopped vegetables or boiled short pasta can be used in the soup, however, they should only be added just before serving.

• Top each bowl of soup with a teaspoon of basil pesto, to make minestrone genovese.

Shredding the cabbage finely

Adding pasta to simmering soup

scotch broth

This soup, a rich lamb stock with root vegetables and barley, can also have 1/2 cup dry white wine added along with the water.

Skimming fat from surface of soup

Adding cabbage and peas to soup

6 lamb neck chops (1kg)
2 litres water (8 cups)
3/4 cup pearl barley (150g)
1 medium brown onion (150g),
    chopped coarsely
2 medium carrots (240g),
    chopped coarsely
1 medium leek (350g),
    chopped coarsely
2 turnips (430g), trimmed,
    chopped coarsely
2 cups loosely packed, finely
    shredded savoy cabbage (160g)
2/3 cup frozen peas (100g)
2 tablespoons coarsely chopped
    fresh flat-leaf parsley

1 Combine lamb, the water and barley in large saucepan. Bring to a boil; simmer, covered, 1 hour, skimming fat from surface occasionally. *[Can be made ahead to this stage. Cover; refrigerate overnight.]*

2 Add onion, carrot, leek and turnip; simmer, covered, about 40 minutes or until vegetables are tender.

3 Remove lamb from soup; remove meat from bones, discard bones, coarsely chop meat.

4 Return lamb to soup with cabbage and peas; cook, uncovered, 10 minutes.

5 Just before serving, stir in parsley.

SERVES 6

per serve 11.9g fat; 1403kJ

serving suggestion Serve with cheese scones.

tip Any root vegetable can be used in this soup.

french onion soup

PREPARATION TIME 25 MINUTES • COOKING TIME 35 MINUTES

This classic soup became famous almost a hundred years ago as the early morning staple of Parisienne workers in Les Halles markets. Its restorative qualities became appreciated among late-night revellers winding down at the markets, then spread to the vast hordes of tourists that descended on the French capital after the war. One of the easiest soups imaginable to make, you'll soon discover why it became – and has remained – so popular.

50g butter
6 medium brown onions (900g), sliced thickly
4 cloves garlic, crushed
1/2 cup dry red wine (125ml)
2 litres beef stock (8 cups)
4 sprigs fresh thyme
2 bay leaves
1 small French bread stick
1 cup coarsely grated gruyère cheese (125g)

Stirring the onion as it caramelises

1 Melt butter in large saucepan; cook onion and garlic, stirring, about 15 minutes or until onion caramelises.

2 Stir in wine, stock, thyme and bay leaves. Bring to a boil; simmer, uncovered, 20 minutes, stirring occasionally. *[Can be made ahead to this stage. Cover; refrigerate overnight or freeze.]*

3 Meanwhile, cut bread into 2cm slices, place bread on oven tray; toast under hot grill until browned lightly both sides. Divide cheese among toasted bread; grill until cheese melts and is browned lightly.

4 Just before serving, divide cheese toasts among serving bowls; pour hot onion soup over the toasts.

SERVES 6

per serve 14.6g fat; 1212kJ

serving suggestion Serve with a fresh baguette and a bottle of red wine.

tips While gruyère is the traditional cheese of choice, you can substitute it with Emmenthaler or Jarlsberg.

• The secret to getting the flavour of this soup right is in the long, slow caramelising of the onion.

pho bo

PREPARATION TIME 30 MINUTES • COOKING TIME 2 HOURS 30 MINUTES

Pronounced "fah bah", this Vietnamese beef noodle soup has assumed cult status in the past decade or so, with restaurants specialising in it opening up throughout the Western world. Many places serve the beef raw, allowing diners to drop it, piece by piece, into the hot broth to cook at the table.

1.5kg beef bones
**2 medium brown onions (300g),
    chopped coarsely**
**2 medium carrots (240g),
    chopped coarsely**
**4 trimmed celery sticks (300g),
    chopped coarsely**
2 cinnamon sticks
4 star anise
6 cardamom pods, bruised
10 black peppercorns
2 tablespoons fish sauce
6 cloves
**60g piece fresh ginger,
    sliced thinly**
6 cloves garlic, sliced thinly
500g piece gravy beef
4 litres water (16 cups)
2 tablespoons soy sauce
200g bean thread vermicelli
100g bean sprouts
**1/2 cup loosely packed fresh
    Vietnamese mint leaves**
4 red Thai chillies, sliced thinly
**1 medium brown onion (150g),
    sliced thinly, extra**
**1/2 cup loosely packed fresh
    coriander leaves**

1 Preheat oven to hot. Combine beef bones, onion, carrot and celery in large baking dish; roast in hot oven, uncovered, about 45 minutes or until browned all over. Drain excess fat from dish.

2 Combine beef mixture, cinnamon, star anise, cardamom, peppercorns, fish sauce, cloves, ginger, garlic, gravy beef and the water in large saucepan. Bring to a boil; simmer, uncovered, 1½ hours, skimming occasionally. Strain through muslin-lined strainer into large bowl. Reserve broth and beef; discard bones and spices. When beef is cool enough to handle, shred finely; return with soy sauce and broth to clean pan. *[Can be made ahead. Cover; refrigerate overnight or freeze.]*

3 Just before serving, place vermicelli in large heatproof bowl; cover with boiling water, stand 3 minutes, drain. Add vermicelli to pan; stir over heat until hot. Serve with sprouts, mint, chilli, extra onion and coriander.

SERVES 6

per serve 5.3g fat; 1000kJ

serving suggestions This soup can be accompanied by more raw greens such as basil leaves, regular garden mint leaves or finely shredded cabbage.

tips Chicken is often substituted for beef in pho recipes.

• Try adding various kinds of offal, like tripe, as do the Vietnamese.

Shredding the cooked gravy beef

turkish yogurt, cucumber and mint soup

PREPARATION TIME 15 MINUTES (plus standing time)
COOKING TIME 25 MINUTES

Along with French and Chinese, Turkish food is regarded as one of the world's three great cuisines, and this unexpected but thoroughly luscious creamy soup will convince you that this claim is correct. Use the thickest, full-cream plain yogurt you can find, preferably one made of sheep milk.

2 litres chicken stock (8 cups)
3/4 cup white long-grain rice (150g)
2 Lebanese cucumbers (260g), seeded, chopped finely
1 teaspoon salt
2 cups yogurt (500ml)
2 eggs
60g butter
2 teaspoons hot paprika
1/3 cup firmly packed fresh mint leaves, shredded finely

Adding hot stock mixture to yogurt mixture

1 Place stock in large saucepan; bring to a boil. Add rice; simmer, uncovered, about 15 minutes or until rice is just tender.

2 Meanwhile, place cucumber in colander; sprinkle with salt, stand 15 minutes. Rinse under cold water; drain on absorbent paper.

3 Whisk yogurt and eggs in large bowl until combined. Gradually add 1 cup of hot stock mixture to yogurt mixture, stirring constantly. Add yogurt mixture to pan containing remainder of the stock; stir constantly over low heat, without boiling, until thickened slightly. Stand 1 hour. Reheat until soup thickens and is heated through.

4 Meanwhile, melt butter in small saucepan; cook paprika, stirring, 2 minutes. Stir in 1 tablespoon of the mint.

5 Just before serving, stir remaining mint into soup. Divide soup among serving bowls; swirl butter mixture into each bowl then top each with a heaped tablespoon of cucumber.

SERVES 6

per serve 13.3g fat; 1341kJ

serving suggestion Accompany this soup with toasted shards of pitta and a bowl of tabbouleh.

tips Do not boil the soup after stock and yogurt are combined or the soup will curdle.

• If you prefer, omit the cucumber and add 100g of finely shredded wilted spinach when you stir in the mint.

borscht

PREPARATION TIME 30 MINUTES • COOKING TIME 1 HOUR 30 MINUTES

One of the most famous of all Russian soups, borscht can be served hot or cold, pureed or chunky, meatless or replete with shredded beef, chicken or pork. This version, a traditional Ukrainian borscht, is based on a strong-flavoured beef stock, acidulated with lemon or vinegar, and always served hot.

2kg bunch fresh beetroot (about 6 beetroot)
50g butter
2 medium brown onions (300g), chopped finely
2 medium potatoes (400g), chopped coarsely
400g can tomatoes
2 medium carrots (240g), chopped coarsely
2.5 litres water (10 cups)
1/3 cup red wine vinegar (80ml)
500g piece gravy beef
3 bay leaves
4 cups shredded savoy cabbage (320g)
1/2 cup sour cream (125ml)
2 tablespoons finely chopped fresh flat-leaf parsley

Coarsely grating beetroot in food processor

1　Discard beetroot leaves and stems; peel and coarsely grate raw beetroot.

2　Melt butter in large saucepan; cook onion, stirring, until soft. Add beetroot, potato, undrained crushed tomatoes, carrot, the water, vinegar, beef and bay leaves. Bring to a boil; simmer, covered, 1 hour. *[Best made ahead to this stage. Cover; refrigerate overnight.]*

3　Remove and discard fat from surface of soup mixture. Remove beef from soup, shred beef then return to soup with cabbage; simmer, uncovered, 20 minutes.

4　Ladle soup into serving bowls; divide sour cream and parsley among bowls.

SERVES 6

per serve 18.8g fat; 1794kJ

serving suggestion Serve with warm homemade potato and caraway bread.

tip　To avoid staining your hands, wear disposable kitchen gloves when peeling beetroot then grate it using a food processor.

chicken and chorizo gumbo

PREPARATION TIME 30 MINUTES • COOKING TIME 2 HOURS 15 MINUTES

Gumbo is the thick, robust soup that's one of the mainstays of Louisiana's Creole cooking – everyone who's ever visited New Orleans will have sampled gumbo. Traditionally made with andouille, a spicy smoked sausage of French descent, gumbo is just as delicious made with the more readily available chorizo.

1.5kg chicken
1 medium brown onion (150g),
   chopped coarsely
2 medium carrots (240g),
   chopped coarsely
2 trimmed celery sticks (150g),
   chopped coarsely
1 bay leaf
12 black peppercorns
3 litres water (12 cups)
60g butter
2 cloves garlic, crushed
1 small brown onion (80g),
   chopped finely
1 medium red capsicum (200g),
   chopped finely
1 teaspoon sweet paprika
1/4 teaspoon ground cayenne
1/4 teaspoon ground clove
2 teaspoons dried oregano
1/4 cup plain flour (35g)
1/4 cup tomato paste (60g)
2 tablespoons Worcestershire sauce
400g can tomatoes
200g fresh okra
1 cup calrose rice (200g)
200g chorizo sausage,
   sliced thinly

1 Rinse chicken under cold water, pat dry with absorbent paper.

2 Combine chicken, medium onion, carrot, celery, bay leaf, peppercorns and the water in large saucepan; bring to a boil. Simmer, covered, 1 1/2 hours, skimming occasionally; strain through muslin-lined strainer into large bowl. Reserve stock and chicken; discard vegetables. *[Can be made ahead to this stage. Cover; refrigerate overnight or freeze.]*

3 When chicken is cool enough to handle, remove and discard skin. Remove chicken meat from carcass; shred meat, discard bones.

4 Melt butter in large saucepan; cook garlic and small onion, stirring, until onion is soft. Add capsicum, paprika, cayenne, clove and oregano; cook, stirring, about 2 minutes or until fragrant.

5 Stir in flour; cook, stirring, until mixture thickens and bubbles. Gradually stir in reserved stock, paste, sauce and undrained crushed tomatoes; stir until mixture boils and thickens. Stir in halved okra and rice; simmer, uncovered, stirring occasionally, about 15 minutes or until both okra and rice are tender.

6 Meanwhile, heat large non-stick frying pan; cook sausage, in batches, until browned, drain on absorbent paper.

7 Add reserved chicken and sausage; stir gumbo over heat until heated through.

SERVES 6

per serve 22.2g fat; 2116kJ

serving suggestion Serve with a fresh, crisp baguette.

tip Fresh rather than canned okra should be used in gumbo (it's used to thicken the soup as well as impart flavour). Choose bright green, small, firm okra pods; large okra are generally tough and stringy. And take great pains not to overcook okra or it will break down to an unpleasantly pulpy state.

Cutting okra in half on the diagonal

Draining chorizo on absorbent paper

pea and ham soup

PREPARATION TIME 15 MINUTES (plus soaking time)
COOKING TIME 1 HOUR 10 MINUTES

Blue boilers – or field peas – are a special variety of pea grown specifically for being dried and used whole; when dried and halved, they're called split peas.

2 cups blue boilers (375g)
**1 medium brown onion (150g),
  chopped coarsely**
**2 trimmed celery sticks (150g),
  chopped coarsely**
2 bay leaves
1.5kg ham bone
2.5 litres water (10 cups)
1 teaspoon cracked black pepper

Shredding ham finely

1 Combine ingredients in large saucepan. Bring to a boil; simmer, covered, about 1 hour or until peas are tender.

2 Remove ham bone; when cool enough to handle, remove ham from bone. Discard bone and fat; shred ham finely.

3 Blend or process half of the pea mixture, in batches, until pureed; return to pan with remaining unprocessed pea mixture and ham. Reheat soup, stirring, over heat until hot. *[Can be made ahead to this stage. Cover; refrigerate overnight or freeze.]*

SERVES 6

per serve 4.2g fat; 1178kJ
serving suggestion Serve with homemade sourdough croutons.
tip Blue boilers do not need to be presoaked before use.

hot and sour soup

PREPARATION TIME 25 MINUTES (plus soaking time)
COOKING TIME 2 HOURS 30 MINUTES

This hot and sour soup originated in the Sichuan province of western China, where it helps lend warmth on cold days. Specifically designed to stimulate the appetite for the meal to come, it is served as a course in itself near the beginning of a meal, immediately after the appetiser.

1.5kg chicken bones
4 litres water (16 cups)
2 medium brown onions (300g),
   chopped coarsely
2 trimmed celery sticks (150g),
   chopped coarsely
1 large carrot (180g),
   chopped coarsely
1 tablespoon Sichuan
   peppercorns
3 bay leaves
340g chicken breast fillets
6 dried shiitake mushrooms
225g can bamboo shoots,
   drained, sliced thinly
50g piece fresh ginger,
   sliced thinly
2 teaspoons sesame oil
2 tablespoons cider vinegar
2 tablespoons sweet
   chilli sauce
1/4 cup soy sauce (60ml)
150g rice stick noodles
4 green onions, sliced thinly

1   Combine chicken bones with the water, brown onion, celery, carrot, peppercorns and bay leaves in large saucepan. Bring to a boil; simmer, uncovered, 1 1/2 hours, skimming occasionally.

2   Add chicken breast; simmer, uncovered, about 20 minutes or until chicken is cooked through. Strain through muslin-lined strainer into large bowl. Reserve stock and chicken; discard bones and vegetables. When chicken is cool enough to handle, shred finely. *[Can be made ahead to this stage. Cover separately; refrigerate overnight or freeze.]*

3   Meanwhile, place mushrooms in small heatproof bowl, cover with boiling water, stand 10 minutes; drain. Remove and discard stems from mushrooms; slice caps thinly.

4   Return stock to same cleaned pan with mushrooms, bamboo shoots, ginger, oil, vinegar and sauces; bring to a boil. Simmer, uncovered, 15 minutes, stirring occasionally. Add shredded chicken and noodles; cook, stirring, about 5 minutes or until noodles are just tender.

5   Just before serving, add green onion to soup.

SERVES 6

per serve 4.5g fat; 686kJ

serving suggestion Serve to start a multi-course Chinese banquet based on the cold-climate recipes of Sichuan or Beijing.

tip Use chicken necks or wings to make the stock rather than the chicken bones.

Shredding the cooled chicken

vichyssoise

PREPARATION TIME 15 MINUTES (plus refrigeration time) • COOKING TIME 40 MINUTES

Vichyssoise is a well-known French potato and leek soup; rich and creamy, it is generally served cold.

60g butter
1 large brown onion (200g),
    chopped finely
2 medium leeks (700g),
    sliced thinly
3 large potatoes (900g),
    chopped coarsely
4 trimmed celery sticks (300g),
    chopped coarsely
2 litres chicken stock (8 cups)
3/4 cup cream (180ml)
2 tablespoons finely chopped
    fresh chervil

1 Melt butter in large saucepan; cook onion, stirring, until onion is soft. Add leek; cook, stirring, about 10 minutes or until leek is soft.

2 Add potato and celery; cook, stirring, 2 minutes. Stir in stock, bring to a boil; simmer, uncovered, about 15 minutes or until potato is soft, stirring occasionally.

3 Blend or process soup, in batches, adding cream gradually, until smoothly pureed. *[Best made ahead to this stage. Cover; refrigerate 3 hours or overnight.]*

4 Just before serving, sprinkle chervil over cold soup.

SERVES 6

per serve 22g fat; 1573kJ

serving suggestion Can be served hot with garlic croutons.

tips Both the leek and potato must be cooked until very soft for the requisite smoothness of this soup.

• We recommend you use homemade stock for this delicate soup; the commercially packaged stocks impart conflicting flavours.

Slicing the white part of each leek thinly

Chopping the fresh chervil finely

manhattan clam chowder

PREPARATION TIME 25 MINUTES • COOKING TIME 25 MINUTES

The word "chowder" comes from chaudière, *the French name for the huge cauldron used on seaport docks by fishermen to stew their fresh catch. Based on tomato, rather than cream, this thick, American seafood chowder is red in colour and thinner than its better-known counterpart, New England clam chowder.*

1.5kg clams
1 cup dry white wine (250ml)
40g butter
1 medium brown onion (150g),
  chopped finely
2 bacon rashers, chopped finely
2 trimmed celery sticks (150g),
  chopped finely
1/4 cup plain flour (35g)
3 cups fish stock (750ml)
400g can tomatoes
3 cups water (750ml)
1 tablespoon fresh thyme leaves
2 bay leaves
4 large potatoes (1.2kg),
  cut into 1cm cubes
1/4 cup loosely packed, coarsely
  chopped fresh flat-leaf parsley

1 Rinse clams under cold water; combine with wine in medium saucepan having a tight-fitting lid. Bring to a boil; steam, covered tightly, about 5 minutes or until clams have opened (discard any that do not). Strain clams over large bowl; reserve 1/4 cup cooking liquid.

2 Melt butter in large saucepan; cook onion, stirring, until soft. Add bacon and celery; cook, stirring, 5 minutes. Add flour; cook, stirring, until mixture thickens and bubbles. Gradually stir in stock, then add undrained crushed tomatoes and the water; cook, stirring, until mixture boils and thickens. Stir in thyme, bay leaves and potato; cook, covered, stirring occasionally, about 15 minutes or until potato is tender.

3 Just before serving, stir clams, reserved cooking liquid and parsley into chowder.

SERVES 6

per serve 8g fat; 1190kJ

serving suggestion This soup is traditionally served with oyster crackers (small round soda biscuits) but give toasted sesame bagel chips a try.

tips Dry red wine can be substituted for the white wine but be certain that whatever wine you use you would also consider drinking.

• Cubed raw potato won't discolour if submerged in cold water until required.

All clams must open after being steamed

avgolemono

PREPARATION TIME 10 MINUTES • COOKING TIME 25 MINUTES

Avgolemono (pronounced ahv-go-leh-mo-no) is both a delicious classic Greek soup and a sauce made up of chicken stock, eggs and lemon juice. The sauce has less stock added so is, naturally, thicker than the soup, while the soup usually has a small amount of white rice added for texture.

2.25 litres chicken stock (9 cups)
1/2 cup white short-grain rice (100g)
3 eggs, separated
1/3 cup lemon juice (80ml)

1 Bring stock to a boil in large saucepan, add rice; cook, stirring occasionally, about 15 minutes or until rice is tender. Reduce heat to lowest possible setting.

2 Working quickly, beat egg whites in small bowl with electric mixer until soft peaks form. Add yolks; continue beating until combined. With motor operating, gradually add lemon juice and 1 cup of the hot stock, beating until combined.

3 Remove stock mixture from heat; gradually add egg mixture, stirring constantly. Serve soup immediately.

SERVES 6

per serve 3.2g fat; 749kJ

serving suggestion Serve as a first course, followed by a Greek braised lamb and vegetable main.

tips The stock mixture must to be taken off the heat before adding the egg mixture or the soup will curdle. There is a belief among Greek cooks that whistling when adding the egg mixture will prevent curdling.

• A cup of finely shredded poached chicken breast meat can be added to this soup, if desired.

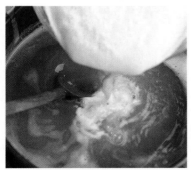

Stirring egg mixture into the stock

japanese dashi broth

PREPARATION TIME 5 MINUTES • COOKING TIME 15 MINUTES

Versions of this soup are eaten every morning by the people of Japan. Some regional versions use buckwheat soba rather than the wheat flour somen noodle, some call for miso to be added to the broth, yet others make it heartier with the addition of finely chopped seasonal vegetables. The basis of this soup is a prepared fish (bonito) stock called dashi, sold in liquid, powdered or granulated form in Asian food shops and many supermarkets. We used dashi granules; if you use powder or liquid, the amount used will have to be adjusted – follow the manufacturer's directions.

100g somen noodles
3 dried shiitake mushrooms
1 lemon
2 teaspoons dashi granules
1.5 litres water (6 cups)
2 tablespoons cooking sake
2 tablespoons mirin
2 tablespoons soy sauce

1 Cook noodles in medium saucepan of boiling water, uncovered, until just tender; drain.

2 Meanwhile, place mushrooms in small heatproof bowl, cover with boiling water, stand until tender; drain, slice thinly.

3 Using vegetable peeler, remove lemon peel in long wide pieces; cut pieces into very thin strips.

4 Combine remaining ingredients in large saucepan; bring to a boil. Simmer stock, uncovered, 10 minutes.

5 Just before serving, divide noodles, mushrooms and lemon among serving bowls; ladle hot dashi into each bowl.

SERVES 6

per serve 0.2g fat; 360kJ

serving suggestion Try serving friends a traditional Japanese breakfast (which includes plain steamed rice, a raw egg, a piece of grilled fish, some pickles and a soup such as this).

tips Of the many possible extra ingredients that can be added to this soup, consider: a few sliced snow peas or green beans; finely grated daikon (Japanese horseradish) or kumara; fresh shiitake mushrooms; shaved wakame or kombu (both dried seaweed); or bean sprouts and tofu.

• If the soup is to kick-start your day, keep it simple; add the solids only if it is to be eaten for lunch or dinner.

Dried mushrooms must be softened in water

tomato and bread soup

PREPARATION TIME 30 MINUTES • COOKING TIME 45 MINUTES

Another Italian favourite, this simple soup hails from Tuscany, a province well known for the wealth of its produce. The more stale the bread, the better it is for this recipe – which should be made close to serving time as it will become stodgy on resting.

100g piece ciabatta
1 tablespoon olive oil
2 large brown onions (400g), chopped finely
3 cloves garlic, crushed
2kg tomatoes, peeled, chopped coarsely
2 litres chicken stock (8 cups)
2 tablespoons tomato paste
1 teaspoon sugar
1/4 cup loosely packed, coarsely chopped fresh basil leaves

1 Cut bread into 2cm slices, place on oven tray; bake, uncovered, in hot oven about 10 minutes or until crisp. *[Can be made ahead to this stage; store up to 2 days in airtight container.]*

2 Heat oil in large saucepan; cook onion and garlic, stirring, until onion is soft. Add tomato; cook, stirring occasionally, about 10 minutes or until tomato is pulpy.

3 Break bread into large pieces directly into pan. Add stock, paste and sugar; simmer, uncovered, about 15 minutes or until soup thickens slightly. Stir occasionally to break up any bread pieces. Just before serving soup, stir in basil.

SERVES 6

per serve 4.3g fat; 862kJ

serving suggestion Drizzled with extra virgin olive oil, this is a good entree before an Italian meat course.

tip Use any leftover stale bread having a hard, crunchy crust if ciabatta is not available.

Slicing ciabatta 2cm thick

Breaking crisp bread directly into soup

tom ka gai

This is the traditional creamy coconut and chicken soup we've all eaten, either in Thailand or at our favourite local Thai restaurant – now you can make it yourself and enjoy it more often.

2 teaspoons peanut oil
1 tablespoon finely chopped lemon grass
1 tablespoon grated fresh galangal
2 teaspoons grated fresh ginger
1 clove garlic, crushed
3 red Thai chillies, seeded, chopped finely
4 kaffir lime leaves, sliced finely
1/4 teaspoon ground turmeric
2²/₃ cups coconut milk (660ml)
1 litre chicken stock (4 cups)
2 cups water (500ml)
1 tablespoon fish sauce
500g chicken thigh fillets, sliced thinly
3 green onions, chopped finely
2 tablespoons lime juice
1 tablespoon coarsely chopped fresh coriander leaves

Finely slicing the kaffir lime leaves

1 Heat oil in large saucepan; cook lemon grass, galangal, ginger, garlic, chilli, lime leaves and turmeric, stirring, about 2 minutes or until fragrant.

2 Stir in coconut milk, stock, the water and fish sauce; bring to a boil. Add chicken; simmer, uncovered, about 20 minutes or until chicken is cooked through and soup liquid reduced slightly.

3 Just before serving, stir onion, juice and coriander into soup.

SERVES 6

per serve 30.8g fat; 1657kJ

serving suggestions Serve with steamed jasmine rice and a side plate of fresh mint leaves, bean sprouts and lime wedges.

tip Remove all excess fat from chicken before cooking.

seafood bisque

PREPARATION TIME 30 MINUTES • COOKING TIME 55 MINUTES

Seafood bisque began life as a waterfront soup – where better is there to source the copious amount of prawn shells required to give this beautiful soup its intense flavour? Nowadays, home cooks replicate the flavours of the sea by making their own bisque base using the shells from the prawns, enriching the liquid with the addition of cream.

300g medium uncooked prawns
2.5 litres fish stock (10 cups)
2 bay leaves
3 sprigs fresh flat-leaf parsley
60g butter
3 small leeks (600g),
**   chopped finely**
1/3 cup plain flour (50g)
1/2 cup brandy (125ml)
1/3 cup lemon juice (80ml)
300g crab meat
1 cup cream (250ml)
1/4 teaspoon ground cayenne
1 tablespoon coarsely
**   chopped fresh dill**

Pushing leek mixture through large sieve

1   Shell and devein prawns, leaving tails intact. Reserve shells; chop prawn meat coarsely.

2   Combine stock, reserved shells, bay leaves and parsley in large saucepan. Bring to a boil; simmer, uncovered, 20 minutes. Strain through muslin-lined strainer into large bowl; discard solids, reserve broth. *[Can be made ahead to this stage. Cover; refrigerate overnight or freeze.]*

3   Melt butter in same cleaned pan; cook leek, stirring, about 10 minutes or until soft. Stir in flour; cook, stirring, until mixture bubbles and thickens. Gradually stir in combined brandy and juice; cook, stirring, until mixture boils and thickens. Using back of spoon, push leek mixture through large sieve into large clean saucepan; discard solids in sieve.

4   Return leek mixture to heat, gradually stirring in the broth; cook, stirring, until mixture boils and thickens. Stir in crab and prawn meat; cook, stirring, 5 minutes. Just before serving, stir cream, cayenne and dill into bisque.

SERVES 6

per serve 24.5g fat; 1567kJ

serving suggestion Serve as the entree of an elegant dinner.

tip Commercially made fish stock can be substituted for the homemade stock, but the prawn shells should still be cooked and strained, as in step 2, for the correct colour and flavour.

mexican tortilla soup

PREPARATION TIME 25 MINUTES (plus soaking time) • COOKING TIME 45 MINUTES

Removing stems from chillies

Processing tomato mixture and chillies

Cutting tortillas into 1cm strips

To prove there's more to Mexican food than that unpalatable fare sold in fast food outlets, this subtle yet full-flavoured broth, a classic Mexican recipe, will whet your appetite. Made in homes all over the country, some tortilla soup versions call for the addition of fresh cheese, cream or chopped avocado. The guajillo *chilli, sometimes called* travieso *("impish", because its heat can be deceiving) or* cascabel *("little bell", because its dried seeds rattle when the chilli is shaken) is the dried form of the fresh* mirasol *chilli. So deep-red in colour it is almost black, the medium-hot guajillo chilli must be soaked in boiling water before being used.*

3 guajillo chillies
3/4 cup boiling water (180ml)
2 teaspoons vegetable oil
1 large brown onion (200g),
  chopped coarsely
3 cloves garlic, crushed
4 medium tomatoes (760g),
  chopped coarsely
1.5 litres chicken stock (6 cups)
2 tablespoons lime juice
2 cups water (500ml), extra
350g chicken breast fillets,
  chopped coarsely
5 corn tortillas
vegetable oil, for shallow-
  frying, extra
1 small red onion (100g),
  chopped finely
1 small avocado (200g),
  chopped finely
1 medium tomato (190g),
  seeded, chopped finely, extra

1 Remove stems from chillies. Place chillies in small heatproof bowl; cover with the water, stand 10 minutes.

2 Meanwhile, heat oil in large saucepan; cook brown onion and garlic, stirring, until onion is soft. Add tomato and undrained chillies; cook, stirring, about 10 minutes or until tomato is pulpy. Blend or process chilli mixture until pureed. *[Can be made ahead to this stage. Cover; refrigerate overnight or freeze.]*

3 Return chilli mixture to same cleaned pan; stir in stock, juice and the extra water. Bring to a boil, add chicken; simmer, uncovered, about 25 minutes or until chicken is cooked through.

4 Meanwhile, slice tortillas into 1cm strips. Heat extra oil in large frying pan; shallow-fry tortilla strips, in batches, until browned lightly. Drain on absorbent paper.

5 Just before serving, divide soup among serving bowls; sprinkle with tortilla strips and combined red onion, avocado and extra tomato.

SERVES 6

per serve 13.4g fat; 1257kJ
serving suggestions Serve as a main dish at lunch with guacamole and warmed flour tortillas.

tips Tortilla strips can be fried a day before required and kept in an airtight container.

• To keep the fat count down, crisp tortilla strips in a hot oven.

• Other dried Mexican chillies can be substituted for the guajillos but the taste of the soup will be different.

chicken noodle soup

PREPARATION TIME 15 MINUTES • COOKING TIME 2 HOURS 45 MINUTES

Immigrants from Eastern Europe to America brought with them the belief that chicken noodle soup was "good for what ails you", and it soon became commonly called Jewish penicillin (a name that exists to this day, as manifestly confirmed in the best-selling series of Chicken Soup for the Soul *books). We actually used tagliatelle in our version of this recipe because its narrow width and delicate texture make it a natural for this healthy soup.*

1.6kg whole chicken
4 litres water (16 cups)
1 medium brown onion (150g), chopped coarsely
2 trimmed celery sticks (150g), chopped coarsely
2 medium carrots (240g), chopped coarsely
2 cloves garlic, crushed
2 bay leaves
10 black peppercorns
1 medium parsnip (125g), chopped coarsely
1 medium turnip (215g), chopped coarsely
125g tagliatelle
2 tablespoons coarsely chopped fresh flat-leaf parsley
1 tablespoon coarsely chopped fresh dill

Skimming fat from surface of broth

1 Combine chicken with the water, onion, celery, carrot, garlic, bay leaves and peppercorns in large saucepan. Bring to a boil; simmer, uncovered, 1½ hours, skimming fat from surface occasionally. Strain through muslin-lined strainer into large bowl; reserve broth, chicken and vegetables, discard bay leaves. When chicken is cool enough to handle, remove and discard skin and bones; chop meat finely. *[Can be made ahead to this stage. Cover; refrigerate overnight or freeze.]*

2 Return chicken, vegetables and broth to same cleaned pan; bring to a boil. Add parsnip and turnip; simmer, uncovered, about 30 minutes or until parsnip and turnip are both tender.

3 Add pasta; cook, stirring, about 10 minutes or until just tender.

4 Just before serving, stir parsley and dill into soup.

SERVES 6

per serve 6.4g fat; 1178kJ

serving suggestion Serve with homemade scones or potato-and-dill bread.

tips Any noodle can be substituted for the tagliatelle: a traditional Eastern European inclusion is *spaetzle* – tiny, wriggly noodles made by pushing a flour, egg and milk batter through a sieve directly into the soup.

• Omit the parsnip and turnip, if desired, and add a cup of shelled fresh baby peas to the soup when you add the pasta.

prawn laksa

PREPARATION TIME 45 MINUTES • COOKING TIME 1 HOUR 20 MINUTES

There are several versions of this Malaysian spicy noodle soup, each of them delicious. Our recipe has its origins in the laksas of Penang, a colonial city on the north-west coast, known for the splendid variety of its seafood. Vietnamese mint leaves are called daun laksa (laksa leaves) in Malaysia, and are an integral ingredient to every laksa.

2kg medium uncooked prawns
1 bunch fresh coriander
   (approximately 100g)
4 trimmed celery sticks (300g),
   chopped coarsely
2 medium carrots (240g),
   chopped coarsely
2 large brown onions (400g),
   chopped coarsely
3 litres water (12 cups)
2 sticks lemon grass,
   chopped coarsely
3 red Thai chillies, seeded,
   chopped coarsely
1 teaspoon ground turmeric
1/4 cup loosely packed,
   coarsely chopped fresh
   Vietnamese mint leaves
2 cloves garlic, crushed
1 tablespoon grated fresh ginger
1 tablespoon grated fresh galangal
1 tablespoon shrimp paste
1 tablespoon ground coriander
2 tablespoons peanut oil
400ml coconut milk
100g fresh Singapore egg noodles
200g fried tofu
100g bean sprouts
4 green onions, sliced thinly

1 Shell and devein prawns; reserve shells. Cut roots from coriander; wash leaves and roots well, reserve both but keep separate.

2 Combine reserved shells, coriander roots, celery, carrot and half of the brown onion with the water in large saucepan. Bring to a boil; simmer, uncovered, 30 minutes. Strain through muslin-lined strainer into large bowl; reserve broth, discard shells and vegetables. *[Can be made ahead to this stage. Cover; refrigerate overnight or freeze.]*

3 Blend or process remaining brown onion with a loosely packed 1/4-cup of the coriander leaves, lemon grass, chilli, turmeric, mint, garlic, ginger, galangal, shrimp paste, ground coriander and half of the oil until mixture forms a paste. *[Can be made ahead to this stage. Cover tightly; refrigerate overnight.]*

4 Heat remaining oil in large saucepan; cook laksa paste, stirring, about 2 minutes or until fragrant. Stir in reserved broth and coconut milk, bring to a boil; simmer, uncovered, 20 minutes. Stir in prawns; cook, stirring, about 10 minutes or until prawns are changed in colour.

5 Meanwhile, place noodles in large heatproof bowl, cover with boiling water; stand 3 minutes, drain. Cut tofu into 2cm cubes.

6 Just before serving, stir noodles, tofu, 2 tablespoons finely chopped coriander leaves, sprouts and green onion into laksa.

SERVES 6

per serve 25.6g fat; 1926kJ

serving suggestion Serve after some steamed pork gow gees.

tip If you don't have access to packages of fried tofu, use fresh – cut tofu into cubes then shallow-fry it in vegetable oil until browned lightly; drain on absorbent paper.

Straining prawn broth through muslin

Processing laksa paste

cuban black bean and lamb soup

PREPARATION TIME 25 MINUTES (plus soaking time) • COOKING TIME 1 HOUR 45 MINUTES

Black beans, also known as turtle beans, are a common ingredient in Latin American soups, salads and salsa. They have a black skin, creamy texture and sweet flavour, and are a breed apart from Chinese black beans which are, in fact, fermented soy beans.

2 cups black beans (400g)
500g boned lamb shoulder
1 tablespoon olive oil
1 large red onion (300g),
   chopped finely
2 cloves garlic, crushed
2 trimmed celery sticks (150g),
   sliced thinly
1 tablespoon ground cumin
1/2 teaspoon ground cayenne
2 1/2 litres water (10 cups)
400g can tomatoes
1/4 cup dry sherry (60ml)
1/4 cup balsamic vinegar (60ml)
1/4 cup loosely packed, coarsely
   chopped fresh coriander leaves
2 limes
4 red Thai chillies, seeded,
   chopped finely
1/3 cup white wine vinegar (80ml)
1/2 cup sour cream (125ml)

Trimming lamb of excess fat

1 Place beans in medium bowl, cover with water; soak overnight, drain.

2 Trim lamb of excess fat; cut lamb into 1.5cm pieces.

3 Heat oil in large saucepan; cook onion and garlic, stirring, until onion is soft. Add lamb, celery, cumin and cayenne; cook, stirring, about 5 minutes or until spices are just fragrant.

4 Stir in the water and undrained crushed tomatoes. Bring to a boil; simmer, covered, 30 minutes. Add beans; simmer, covered, about 1 hour or until beans are tender. Stir in sherry and balsamic vinegar; cool 10 minutes.

5 Blend or process half of the soup, in batches, until pureed. *[Can be made ahead to this stage. Cover; refrigerate overnight.]*

6 Combine pureed soup with coriander and remaining soup in pan; stir over heat until hot.

7 Meanwhile, cut limes into wedges. Combine chilli and wine vinegar in small bowl. Serve soup accompanied by lime wedges, chilli mixture and sour cream.

SERVES 6

per serve 18.8g fat; 1760kJ
serving suggestion Serve with freshly made jalapeño corn bread.

tips You can substitute gravy beef (or better yet, a ham bone and chicken stock) for the lamb.

• Some Cubans like it hot: add 2 finely chopped Thai chillies with the other spices if you do too.

gazpacho

PREPARATION TIME 30 MINUTES (plus refrigeration time)

A chilled soup originating in the southern province of Andalusia in Spain, gazpacho, like other peasant soups, makes clever use of yesterday's bread and the garden's overripe vegetables.

1 litre tomato juice (4 cups)
10 medium egg tomatoes (750g), chopped coarsely
2 medium red onions (340g), chopped coarsely
2 cloves garlic, quartered
1 Lebanese cucumber (130g), chopped coarsely
2 tablespoons sherry vinegar
1 medium red capsicum (200g), chopped coarsely
1 small red onion (100g), chopped finely, extra
1 Lebanese cucumber (130g), chopped finely, extra
1 small red capsicum (150g), chopped finely, extra
1 tablespoon finely chopped fresh dill

Finely chopping fresh dill

1 Blend or process juice, tomato, onion, garlic, cucumber, vinegar and capsicum, in batches, until pureed. Cover; refrigerate 3 hours. *[Can be made ahead to this stage. Cover; refrigerate overnight or freeze.]*

2 Just before serving, divide soup among serving bowls; stir equal amounts of extra onion, extra cucumber, extra capsicum and dill into each bowl.

SERVES 6

per serve 0.4g fat; 366kJ

serving suggestion To make this soup a complete meal, add 1/2 cup of both finely chopped raw celery and finely chopped green capsicum to the soup, then top each serving with 1 tablespoon of finely diced hard-boiled egg and a few croutons.

tips A finely chopped red chilli added to the blender or processor makes a spicier gazpacho.

• Red wine vinegar can be used instead of sherry vinegar.

chickpea and chorizo soup

This recipe is based on the traditional Portuguese caldo verde, literally, green soup. While the usual "green" ingredient is kale, we have used spinach in our recipe. If you can find garlic-loaded linguiça (Portuguese sausage), use it rather than the more readily available chorizo. The basics of this soup must be assembled, cooked and refrigerated overnight for the flavour to develop.

1 tablespoon olive oil
1 large brown onion (200g),
   chopped finely
2 cloves garlic, crushed
200g chorizo sausage,
   sliced thinly
3 litres water (12 cups)
500g ham bone
4 bay leaves
12 sprigs fresh flat-leaf parsley
1 litre water (4 cups), extra
2 large potatoes (600g),
   chopped coarsely
2 x 300g cans chickpeas,
   drained, rinsed
1 cup firmly packed, finely
   shredded fresh spinach leaves

Using fingers to shred ham finely

1 Heat oil in large saucepan; cook onion and garlic, stirring, until onion is soft. Add sausage; cook, stirring, until sausage is browned. Stir in the water, ham bone, bay leaves and parsley; bring to a boil. Simmer, covered, 1^{1}/2 hours; cool slightly then refrigerate soup mixture, covered, overnight. *[Can also be covered and frozen at this stage.]*

2 Remove and discard fat from surface of soup mixture. Remove ham from bone; discard bone and fat, shred ham finely.

3 Combine soup mixture with the extra water in large saucepan; bring to a boil. Stir in ham and potato; simmer, covered, about 15 minutes or until potato is tender.

4 Add chickpeas to soup; simmer, uncovered, 5 minutes. Just before serving soup, stir in spinach.

SERVES 6

per serve 13.8g fat; 1320kJ
serving suggestions A hearty peasant loaf of bread and a glass of red wine are perfect accompaniments to this soup.

tips Canned haricot or kidney beans, drained and rinsed, can be substituted for the chickpeas.

• Look for linguiça at South American butchers as well as specialist delicatessens.

modern

Creativity comes into play in this chapter: we've loosened the restraints of the classics and launched into a brave new world of different ingredient combinations, tastes and textures. The results are so delicious, exciting and satisfying that we think these soups will become timeless favourites in the future.

roast baby-turnip soup

PREPARATION TIME 25 MINUTES • COOKING TIME 1 HOUR 10 MINUTES

Combining turnips and oil in baking dish

Finely chopping chervil

3kg baby turnips (approximately 4 bunches)
2 tablespoons olive oil
1 large brown onion (200g), chopped coarsely
1 clove garlic, quartered
2 litres chicken stock (8 cups)
1/2 cup cream (125ml)
1/4 cup loosely packed, finely chopped fresh chervil

1 Preheat oven to hot. Trim and discard turnip leaves; leave 3cm-length stem attached to 24 of the smallest turnips, remove and discard stems on remainder. Scrub turnips thoroughly; peel the 24 small turnips, retaining the 3cm stem. Chop remaining unpeeled turnips coarsely.

2 Combine all turnips with half of the oil in large baking dish; toss to coat thoroughly. Roast, uncovered, in hot oven about 45 minutes or until turnips are tender and browned all over.

3 Heat remaining oil in large saucepan; cook onion and garlic, stirring, until onion softens. Add chopped turnip and stock; bring to a boil. Simmer, uncovered, 10 minutes.

4 Blend or process soup mixture, in batches, until pureed. *[Can be made ahead to this stage. Cover; refrigerate overnight.]*

5 Return soup to same cleaned pan with whole turnips and cream; stir over heat until hot. Just before serving, stir in chervil.

SERVES 6

per serve 15.7g fat; 1238kJ

serving suggestion Cheese toast is a delicious accompaniment to this soup.

tip Choose 24 of the smallest turnips you have, matching them as closely as possible in size. Spoon four of these tiny roasted turnips into each portion of soup when serving.

lemony spinach soup with fetta

PREPARATION TIME 25 MINUTES • COOKING TIME 30 MINUTES

40g butter
1 medium brown onion (150g),
 chopped coarsely
4 green onions,
 chopped coarsely
2 cloves garlic, quartered
1 tablespoon coarsely grated
 lemon rind
1.5kg spinach, trimmed,
 chopped coarsely
3 large potatoes (900g),
 chopped coarsely
3 cups vegetable stock (750ml)
1.25 litres water (5 cups)
3/4 cup cream (180ml)
150g fetta, crumbled

1 Melt butter in large saucepan; cook combined onions and garlic, stirring, until onions soften. Add rind, spinach and potato; cook, stirring, until spinach is just wilted.

2 Stir in stock and the water. Bring to a boil; simmer, covered, about 15 minutes or until potato softens.

3 Blend or process soup mixture, in batches, until smooth. *[Can be made ahead to this stage. Cover; refrigerate overnight or freeze.]*

4 Return soup with cream to same cleaned pan; stir over heat until hot. Divide soup among serving bowls; top each with fetta.

SERVES 6

per serve 23g fat; 1395kJ

serving suggestion Serve with a rustic country loaf, kalamata olives and teardrop tomatoes.

tip Parmesan cheese can be substituted for fetta. Use a vegetable peeler to shave parmesan cheese into long, thin strips.

Crumbling the fetta into fairly small chunks

broad bean and corn soup

PREPARATION TIME 25 MINUTES • COOKING TIME 35 MINUTES

1.5kg broad beans, shelled
6 fresh corn cobs
   (approximately 2.5kg)
1 large carrot (180g)
1 tablespoon peanut oil
1¹/₂ tablespoons grated ginger
3 cloves garlic, crushed
2 litres chicken stock (8 cups)
1¹/₂ tablespoons soy sauce
2 green onions, sliced thinly
¹/₂ cup bean sprouts (40g)

1 Boil, steam or microwave beans until just tender. Drain; refresh under cold water then remove and discard outer skins.

2 Cut corn kernels from cobs; cut carrot into matchstick-size pieces.

3 Heat oil in large saucepan; cook ginger and garlic, stirring, 1 minute. Add stock and sauce, bring to a boil. Add beans and corn; cook, uncovered, about 5 minutes or until corn is tender.

4 Just before serving, stir onion and sprouts into soup.

SERVES 6

per serve 6.5g fat; 1499kJ

serving suggestion Serve soup with a watercress salad dressed in a soy-lime vinaigrette.

tip A 500g packet of frozen broad beans can be substituted for the fresh beans, but you must first thaw the frozen beans and remove and discard their beige-coloured skin.

Peeling beige skin from broad beans

chilli chicken and corn soup

PREPARATION TIME 10 MINUTES • COOKING TIME 20 MINUTES

2 tablespoons olive oil
340g chicken breast fillets
1 medium red onion (170g), chopped finely
1 tablespoon plain flour
1.5 litres chicken stock (6 cups)
2 cups tomato juice (500ml)
420g can corn kernels, drained
2 red Thai chillies, seeded, chopped finely
1/4 cup loosely packed fresh coriander leaves

1 Heat half of the oil in large saucepan. Cook chicken until cooked through; when cool enough to handle, shred into small pieces.

2 Heat remaining oil in same pan; cook onion, stirring, until soft. Add flour; cook, stirring, until mixture bubbles and thickens. Gradually stir in stock and juice; cook, stirring, until mixture boils and thickens.

3 Add chicken, corn and chilli; stir over heat until soup is hot. Just before serving soup, stir in coriander.

SERVES 6

per serve 8.5g fat; 1054kJ

serving suggestion This soup makes a lively beginning to a Mexican meal.

tip A purchased barbecued chicken can be substituted for the chicken breasts; discard skin, excess fat and all bones before shredding the meat.

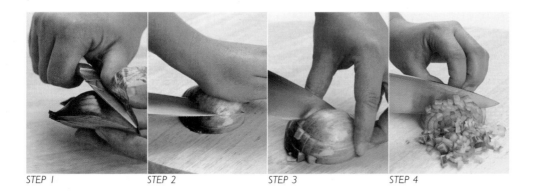

STEP I   STEP 2   STEP 3   STEP 4

How to chop an onion
Halve onion lengthways, leaving root end intact, then peel.
Press onion firmly on board, cut-side down; cut into 2 or 3 slices across.
Gripping onion, slice lengthways as thinly as possible.
Last, cut onion in crosshatch pattern into a fine dice.

curried cauliflower and coriander soup

PREPARATION TIME 20 MINUTES • COOKING TIME 30 MINUTES

1 tablespoon peanut oil
1 large brown onion (200g),
chopped coarsely
2 cloves garlic, quartered
1 tablespoon grated fresh ginger
1 red Thai chilli, seeded,
chopped coarsely
2 teaspoons black mustard seeds
2 teaspoons garam masala
1 teaspoon ground turmeric
2 teaspoons ground cumin
2 teaspoons ground coriander
1.5kg cauliflower, trimmed,
chopped coarsely
1.5 litres chicken stock (6 cups)
1 cup coconut cream (250ml)
1/4 cup plain yogurt (60ml)
1 tablespoon coarsely chopped
fresh coriander leaves

Removing core from cauliflower

Returning the pureed soup to pan

1 Heat oil in large saucepan; cook onion, garlic, ginger and chilli, stirring, until onion softens. Stir in seeds, garam masala and ground spices; cook, stirring, until fragrant. Add cauliflower and stock; bring to a boil. Simmer, uncovered, about 15 minutes or until cauliflower is tender.

2 Blend or process half of the soup mixture, in batches, until pureed. *[Can be made ahead to this stage. Cover; refrigerate overnight or freeze.]*

3 Return pureed soup to pan with remaining unprocessed soup mixture; stir over heat until hot.

4 Just before serving soup, stir in coconut cream, yogurt and coriander leaves.

SERVES 6

per serve 13.1g fat 958kJ
serving suggestion Serve with crisp pappadums.

tip Finely chopped kumara or pumpkin can be substituted for the cauliflower, but the cooking time will change.

potato and fennel soup

PREPARATION TIME 25 MINUTES • COOKING TIME 45 MINUTES

1 tablespoon olive oil
1 medium brown onion (150g),
   chopped coarsely
1 clove garlic, quartered
2 medium fennel bulbs (1kg),
   chopped coarsely
500g ham bones
5 medium potatoes (1kg),
   chopped coarsely
2 litres vegetable stock (8 cups)
1 litre water (4 cups)
6 slices prosciutto (90g)
2 teaspoons finely chopped
   fresh dill

1 Heat oil in large saucepan; cook onion and garlic, stirring, until onion softens. Add fennel; cook, stirring, about 5 minutes or until fennel softens. Add ham bones and potato; cook, stirring, 2 minutes.

2 Add stock and the water; bring to a boil. Simmer, uncovered, about 30 minutes or until potato softens.

3 Remove ham bones from soup when cool enough to handle; remove ham from bones, discard excess fat and bones. Chop ham coarsely; reserve.

4 Cook prosciutto in dry heated non-stick frying pan until crisp; drain on absorbent paper, break into large pieces.

5 Blend or process soup mixture, in batches, until pureed. *[Can be made ahead to this stage. Cover; refrigerate overnight.]*

6 Return soup with ham to same cleaned pan; stir over heat until hot. Just before serving soup, stir in dill and prosciutto chips.

SERVES 6

Breaking crisped prosciutto into pieces

Trimming and chopping the fennel bulb

per serve 8.1g fat; 1236kJ

serving suggestion Accompany soup with olive tapenade on toast.

tip After peeling and chopping potato, submerge in cold water to stop discolouration.

indian dhal and carrot soup

PREPARATION TIME 10 MINUTES • COOKING TIME 50 MINUTES

1 tablespoon peanut oil
1 medium brown onion (150g), chopped coarsely
2 cloves garlic, crushed
1 tablespoon ground cumin
1 tablespoon ground coriander
2 teaspoons garam masala
5 medium carrots (600g), chopped coarsely
2 litres vegetable stock (8 cups)
1.5 litres water (6 cups)
1/2 cup brown lentils (100g)
1/2 cup yellow split peas (100g)
1/2 cup red lentils (100g)
2 tablespoons coarsely chopped fresh coriander leaves

Adding the red lentils to pan

1 Heat oil in large saucepan; cook onion and garlic, stirring, until onion softens. Stir in cumin, coriander and garam masala; cook, stirring, until fragrant. Add carrot; cook, stirring, 2 minutes.

2 Stir in stock and the water; bring to a boil. Add brown lentils and peas; simmer, uncovered, 30 minutes. *[Can be made ahead to this stage. Cover; refrigerate overnight or freeze.]*

3 Add red lentils; simmer, uncovered, about 10 minutes or until both lentils and peas are tender. Just before serving soup, stir in coriander leaves.

SERVES 6

per serve 5.2g fat; 1073kJ

serving suggestion A delicious accompaniment to this soup is garlic naan.

tip A cup each of finely chopped raw potato and pumpkin could be added to the pan at the same time as the brown lentils and peas, if desired.

brussels sprouts soup

PREPARATION TIME 20 MINUTES • COOKING TIME 45 MINUTES

350g brussels sprouts
(approximately 15)
1 teaspoon caraway seeds
500g potatoes, chopped coarsely
2¹/₃ cups milk (580ml)
40g butter
1 medium leek (350g), sliced
2 cloves garlic, crushed
1.25 litres chicken
stock (5 cups)
1 tablespoon lemon juice

1 Remove three good outer leaves from each sprout. Place leaves in small heatproof bowl, cover with boiling water; stand 2 minutes, drain. Place leaves in small bowl of iced water; stand 5 minutes, drain. Reserve leaves.

2 Cut remaining part of each sprout in half. Place seeds in centre of small piece of clean muslin; tie tightly with kitchen string to secure parcel.

3 Combine potato, milk and seed parcel in medium saucepan; bring to a boil. Simmer, uncovered, about 10 minutes or until potato softens. Cool 10 minutes; remove and discard seed parcel.

4 Melt butter in large saucepan; cook leek and garlic, stirring, until leek softens. Add halved sprouts and stock; bring to a boil. Simmer, uncovered, about 10 minutes or until sprout halves soften; stir in potato mixture.

5 Blend or process soup, in batches, until smooth. Return soup to same cleaned pan with juice; stir over heat until hot. Divide soup among serving bowls; top each with reserved leaves.

SERVES 6

per serve 9.7g fat; 949kJ

serving suggestion This soup is great accompanied by sliced ham and Dijon mustard on vienna bread.

tip Brussels sprouts can be kept under refrigeration, sealed in a plastic bag, up to 3 days.

Removing a few leaves from each sprout

jerusalem artichoke and smoked trout soup

PREPARATION TIME 30 MINUTES • COOKING TIME 1 HOUR 15 MINUTES

Crème fraîche is a commercially soured, mature thick cream; substitute sour cream, if preferred. Pick over the trout and discard even the most minuscule bone fragments.

¼ cup olive oil (60ml)
1kg small fresh Jerusalem artichokes (approximately 32), trimmed, peeled
20g butter
3 shallots, chopped coarsely
1 clove garlic, quartered
2 litres chicken stock (8 cups)
2 tablespoons lemon juice
½ cup crème fraîche (125ml)
1 medium smoked trout (375g), flaked
1 tablespoon finely grated lemon rind

1 Preheat oven to hot.

2 Combine oil and artichokes in large baking dish; toss artichokes to coat with oil. Roast in hot oven, uncovered, turning occasionally, about 1 hour or until artichokes are tender.

3 Melt butter in large saucepan; cook shallot and garlic, stirring, until both just soften. Add artichokes, stock and juice; bring to a boil. Simmer, uncovered, 10 minutes; cool 10 minutes.

4 Blend or process soup mixture, in batches, until smooth. *[Can be made ahead to this stage. Cover; refrigerate overnight.]*

5 Return soup to same cleaned pan; stir over heat until hot. Stir in crème fraîche and trout then divide soup among serving bowls; sprinkle each with rind.

SERVES 6

per serve 24g fat; 1522kJ

serving suggestion This soup makes a perfect main meal, accompanied by fresh bread and a green salad.

tip Jerusalem artichokes, available in autumn and winter, can be kept, sealed tightly in a plastic bag in the refrigerator, for about a fortnight.

Trimming and peeling artichokes

Picking out bones, then flaking smoked trout

moroccan chicken and chickpea soup

PREPARATION TIME 20 MINUTES • COOKING TIME 50 MINUTES

2 tablespoons olive oil
340g chicken breast fillets
1 large brown onion (200g), chopped finely
2 cloves garlic, crushed
1 tablespoon grated fresh ginger
1¹/₂ teaspoons ground cumin
1¹/₂ teaspoons ground coriander
1 teaspoon ground turmeric
¹/₂ teaspoon sweet paprika
1 cinnamon stick
¹/₄ cup plain flour (35g)
1 litre chicken stock (4 cups)
1 litre water (4 cups)
2 x 300g cans chickpeas, drained, rinsed
2 x 400g cans tomatoes
2 tablespoons finely chopped preserved lemon
1 tablespoon coarsely chopped fresh coriander leaves

Pinching skin off chickpeas

Finely chopping preserved lemon

1 Heat half of the oil in large frying pan; cook chicken, uncovered, about 10 minutes or until browned both sides and cooked through. Drain chicken on absorbent paper, cool 10 minutes; using two forks, shred chicken coarsely.

2 Heat remaining oil in large saucepan; cook onion, garlic and ginger, stirring, until onion softens. Add cumin, ground coriander, turmeric, paprika and cinnamon; cook, stirring, until fragrant.

3 Add flour; cook, stirring, until mixture bubbles and thickens. Gradually stir in stock and the water; cook, stirring, until mixture comes to a boil. Simmer, uncovered, 20 minutes.

4 Add chickpeas and undrained crushed tomatoes, bring to a boil; simmer, uncovered, 10 minutes. *[Can be made ahead to this stage. Cover; refrigerate overnight.]*

5 Add chicken and lemon; stir over heat until soup is hot. Just before serving soup, stir in fresh coriander.

SERVES 6

per serve 11.3g fat; 1205kJ

serving suggestion Serve with a large bowl of freshly made fattoush.

tip Removing the skin from the chickpeas is not essential, but it gives them a smoother texture.

broccoli and blue cheese soup

PREPARATION TIME 15 MINUTES • COOKING TIME 30 MINUTES

Crumbling the blue cheese

1 tablespoon olive oil
1 large brown onion (200g),
   chopped coarsely
2 medium potatoes (400g),
   chopped coarsely
500g broccoli, trimmed, chopped
2 litres chicken stock (8 cups)
1/2 cup cream (125ml)
150g mild blue cheese, crumbled

1   Heat oil in large saucepan; cook onion, stirring, until soft. Add potato and broccoli; cook, stirring, 2 minutes.

2   Add stock, bring to a boil; simmer, uncovered, about 15 minutes or until potato is tender.

3   Blend or process soup mixture, in batches, until pureed. *[Can be made ahead to this stage. Cover, refrigerate overnight.]*

4   Return soup to same cleaned pan with cream and half of the cheese; stir over heat until hot. Divide soup among serving bowls; sprinkle with remaining cheese.

SERVES 6

per serve   21g fat; 1415kJ

serving suggestion   Accompany this soup with almond and dried fig bread.

tip   Locally made chevre (goat milk cheese) can be substituted for the blue cheese.

⊔ppa primavera

*ɔup emulates the classic Italian primavera, a creamy, spring-vegetable pasta
. We used farfalle (bow-tie) pasta but any short pasta will perform just as well.*

2 tablespoons olive oil
1 medium leek (350g), sliced
2 cloves garlic, crushed
1 tablespoon plain flour
3 cups vegetable stock (750ml)
1.5 litres water (6 cups)
100g squash, chopped coarsely
150g uncooked farfalle pasta
500g fresh asparagus,
    cut into 2cm lengths
100g snow peas, halved
100g sugar snap peas, halved
300ml cream
3 green onions, sliced diagonally

1 Heat oil in large saucepan; cook leek and garlic, stirring, about 5 minutes or until leek softens. Add flour; cook, stirring, until mixture bubbles and thickens. Gradually stir in stock; cook, stirring, until mixture boils and thickens slightly. Add the water, squash and pasta; cook, uncovered, about 10 minutes or until both are just tender.

2 Stir in asparagus and both peas; cook, uncovered, about 5 minutes or until asparagus is just tender.

3 Just before serving, add cream and onion; stir soup over heat until hot.

SERVES 6

per serve 28.5g fat; 1662kJ
serving suggestion Serve with warm ciabatta and a platter of roasted tomatoes.

tips Watch the cooking time and test the pasta and squash occasionally to make certain that neither overcooks.

• After snapping the woody ends off each asparagus spear, peel the remaining lower part to make the spear easy to bite through.

Peeling lower half of asparagus spears

Adding pasta to soup

roast capsicum and tomato soup

PREPARATION TIME 35 MINUTES • COOKING TIME 1 HOUR 10 MINUTES

STEP 1

STEP 2

STEP 3

STEP 4

4 large red capsicums (1.4kg)
1 tablespoon olive oil
1 large red onion (300g),
**   chopped coarsely**
2 cloves garlic, quartered
1kg medium tomatoes, chopped
2 red Thai chillies, seeded,
**   chopped coarsely**
1 litre chicken stock (4 cups)
1 tablespoon balsamic vinegar

PARMESAN WAFERS

1 cup self-raising flour (150g)
80g butter
1 cup finely grated parmesan
**   cheese (80g)**
1 egg yolk
2 tablespoons iced water

1 Quarter capsicums, remove and discard seeds and membranes. Roast under grill or in very hot oven, skin-side up, until skin blisters and blackens; cover capsicum pieces in plastic or paper for 5 minutes, peel away skin. Chop half of the capsicum coarsely; chop remaining capsicum finely.

2 Heat oil in large saucepan; cook onion and garlic, stirring, until onion softens. Add coarsely chopped capsicum, tomato and chilli; cook, stirring, about 10 minutes or until tomato is pulpy.

3 Add stock and vinegar, bring to a boil; simmer, covered, 20 minutes.

4 Blend or process soup mixture, in batches, until smooth. *[Can be made ahead to this stage. Cover; refrigerate overnight.]*

5 Return soup mixture to same cleaned pan with remaining capsicum; stir over heat until hot. Serve soup with parmesan wafers.

parmesan wafers Preheat oven to moderate. Process flour, butter and two-thirds of the cheese until just combined; add egg yolk and the water, process until dough just clings together. Knead dough on floured surface until smooth. Cover; refrigerate 30 minutes. Roll dough between two sheets of baking paper to 3mm thickness; cut dough into 7cm strips, cut strips into triangles. Place triangles on baking-paper-lined oven trays, sprinkle with remaining cheese; bake, uncovered, in moderate oven about 15 minutes or until browned lightly.

SERVES 6

per serve 20.5g fat; 1661kJ
serving suggestion Serve as an entree to a simple roast dinner.

tip Cut parmesan dough into 6cm circles before baking; bake as above then serve topped with additional roasted capsicum, marinated in olive oil and herbs, as part of an antipasti platter.

Roasting capsicum
Quarter each capsicum, then remove and discard all seeds and membranes.
Roast capsicum pieces, skin-side up, in hot oven until blistered and blackened.
Remove from oven; place capsicum pieces in airtight bag for 5 minutes.
Using a sharp knife, carefully lift, peel away and discard the capsicum skin.

buttered cabbage soup with caraway croutons

PREPARATION TIME 25 MINUTES • COOKING TIME 25 MINUTES

40g butter
2 medium brown onions (300g),
    chopped finely
2 cloves garlic, crushed
4 cups shredded savoy
    cabbage (320g)
4 medium potatoes (800g),
    chopped coarsely
3 cups vegetable stock (750ml)
1.5 litres water (6 cups)
250g piece wholemeal bread
¹/₄ cup olive oil (60ml)
1 tablespoon caraway seeds
¹/₂ cup sour cream (125ml)

1 Melt butter in large saucepan; cook onion and garlic, stirring, until onion softens. Add cabbage and potato; cook, stirring, until cabbage is wilted.

2 Preheat oven to hot. Stir in stock and the water. Bring to a boil; simmer, covered, about 20 minutes or until potato softens.

3 Meanwhile, cut bread into 2cm cubes; combine with oil and seeds in large baking dish. Toast, uncovered, stirring occasionally, in hot oven about 15 minutes or until croutons are browned lightly and crisp.

4 Blend or process soup mixture, in batches, until smooth. *[Can be made ahead to this stage. Cover; refrigerate overnight.]*

5 Return soup with cream to same cleaned pan; stir over heat until hot. Divide soup among serving bowls; top each with caraway croutons.

SERVES 6

per serve 25.1g fat; 1822kJ

serving suggestion This soup is the perfect entree for a main course of grilled pork chops and a simple salad.

tip Any type of bread can be substituted for wholemeal (sourdough is particularly good), and either crushed garlic or freshly cracked black pepper can be substituted for the caraway seeds.

Combining oil, bread and seeds in baking dish

eggplant soup with yogurt

4 medium eggplants (1.2kg)
1 tablespoon olive oil
4 cloves garlic, quartered
2 teaspoons ground cumin
1.25 litres vegetable
   stock (5 cups)
1¹/₂ cups water (375ml)
1 tablespoon tahini
2 tablespoons lemon juice
¹/₂ cup plain yogurt (125ml)
¹/₄ cup loosely packed,
   finely chopped fresh chives

1 Preheat oven to moderate.

2 Place eggplants on greased oven tray; pierce all over with skewer or fork. Roast eggplant in moderate oven, uncovered, about 1 hour or until soft. When cool enough to handle, peel eggplant; discard skin, chop flesh coarsely.

3 Heat oil in large saucepan; cook garlic and cumin, stirring, until fragrant. Stir in eggplant, stock and the water. Bring to a boil; simmer, uncovered, 5 minutes.

4 Blend or process eggplant mixture, in batches, until pureed. *[Can be made ahead to this stage. Cover; refrigerate overnight or freeze.]*

5 Return soup mixture with tahini and lemon juice to same cleaned pan; stir over heat until hot. Divide soup among serving bowls; divide yogurt among bowls then sprinkle each with chives.

SERVES 6

per serve 5.7g fat; 498kJ

serving suggestion Serve with toasted pide and a bowl of cracked green olives.

tip The eggplant's bitter juices do not need to be drained away when eggplant is roasted in the oven.

Peeling roasted eggplant

chicken and vegetable soup

PREPARATION TIME 25 MINUTES • COOKING TIME 3 HOURS

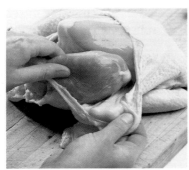
Removing skin from chicken before cooking

Straining stock through muslin

Chopping chicken meat coarsely

1.8kg chicken
1 medium carrot (120g), chopped coarsely
2 trimmed celery sticks (150g), chopped coarsely
1 medium brown onion (150g), chopped coarsely
1 bay leaf
1 teaspoon black peppercorns
3 litres water (12 cups)
1 tablespoon vegetable oil
1 large swede (450g), chopped coarsely
2 large parsnips (360g), chopped finely
1 medium leek (350g), chopped finely
3 trimmed celery sticks (225g), chopped finely, extra
2 medium carrots (240g), chopped finely, extra
2 tablespoons coarsely chopped fresh parsley

1 Remove and discard skin from chicken.

2 Combine chicken with carrot, celery, onion, bay leaf, peppercorns and the water in large saucepan, bring to a boil; simmer, uncovered, 2 hours.

3 Remove chicken from pan; strain vegetable mixture through muslin-lined sieve over large bowl. Discard vegetables; reserve stock. Remove meat from chicken, discard bones; chop chicken meat coarsely. *[Can be made ahead to this stage. Cover separately; freeze or refrigerate overnight.]*

4 Skim away and discard solidified fat from surface of stock.

5 Heat oil in large saucepan; cook remaining vegetables, stirring, about 5 minutes or until leek is soft. Add stock, bring to a boil; simmer, covered, about 45 minutes or until vegetables are just tender. Return chicken to pan with parsley; simmer, uncovered, about 5 minutes or until heated through.

SERVES 8

per serve 10.8g fat; 1207kJ

serving suggestion Serve with homemade mini-dampers.

tip It's easier to remove the meat from a chicken carcass when the chicken is still warm.

swiss brown mushroom soup with garlic croutons

PREPARATION TIME 20 MINUTES • COOKING TIME 40 MINUTES

250g piece ciabatta
1/4 cup olive oil (60ml)
3 cloves garlic, crushed
1 tablespoon olive oil, extra
1 medium brown onion (150g),
   chopped coarsely
1 clove garlic crushed, extra
500g Swiss brown
   mushrooms, halved
2 litres beef stock (8 cups)
1/2 cup dry white wine (125ml)
1 litre water (4 cups)
1 cup cream (250ml)
1 tablespoon coarsely chopped
   fresh tarragon leaves

1 Preheat oven to moderately hot. Cut bread into 2cm cubes; combine with oil and garlic in large bowl, mix well. Place bread in single layer on oven tray; toast, uncovered, stirring occasionally, in moderately hot oven about 20 minutes or until browned lightly and crisp.

2 Heat extra oil in large saucepan; cook onion and extra garlic, stirring, until onion softens. Add mushrooms; cook, stirring, about 5 minutes or until browned lightly. Stir in stock, wine and the water. Bring to a boil; simmer, uncovered, 30 minutes.

3 Blend or process soup mixture, in batches, until smooth. *[Can be made ahead to this stage. Cover; refrigerate overnight.]*

4 Return soup with cream and tarragon to same cleaned pan; stir over heat until hot. Divide soup among serving bowls; top each with garlic croutons.

SERVES 6

per serve 32g fat; 1916kJ
serving suggestion Serve with butter lettuce, avocado and celery salad, sprinkled with toasted pecans.

tip Any kind of bread can be used for croutons; rye or whole grain bread are tasty possibilities.

Mixing bread cubes with oil and garlic

mediterranean lentil soup

PREPARATION TIME 15 MINUTES • COOKING TIME 1 HOUR 25 MINUTES

1/4 cup olive oil (60ml)
1 large brown onion (200g),
  chopped coarsely
1 medium eggplant
  (300g), quartered
4 medium tomatoes
  (760g), quartered
1 large red capsicum
  (350g), quartered
3 cloves garlic, peeled
2 litres vegetable
  stock (8 cups)
1 cup puy lentils (200g)
1/2 cup sour cream (125ml)
2 tablespoons finely
  chopped fresh chives

1 Preheat oven to hot.

2 Combine oil, onion, eggplant, tomato, capsicum and garlic in large baking dish; roast, uncovered, in hot oven about 45 minutes or until vegetables are tender. Turn once midway through cooking time.

3 Place capsicum pieces on plate, skin-side up; cover, stand 5 minutes. Peel capsicum; discard skin, chop flesh coarsely. Peel tomato; discard skin, chop flesh coarsely. Peel eggplant; discard skin, chop flesh coarsely.

4 Blend or process eggplant with garlic and onion until pureed; combine with stock and lentils in large saucepan. Bring to a boil; simmer, uncovered, about 35 minutes or until lentils are tender. *[Can be made ahead to this stage. Cover; refrigerate overnight.]*

5 Add capsicum and tomato; stir over heat until hot. Divide soup among serving bowls; dollop each with sour cream, sprinkle with chives.

SERVES 6

per serve 19.2g fat; 1409kJ
serving suggestion Serve with garlic foccacia.

tip Substitute brown lentils for puy, although they require longer cooking, and use red onion in place of brown onion, if you prefer.

Peeling roasted capsicum

fresh tomato and fennel soup

PREPARATION TIME 20 MINUTES • COOKING TIME 40 MINUTES

STEP 1

STEP 2

STEP 3

STEP 4

This refreshing soup is light enough to serve as a first course when entertaining. Since it freezes so well, make a double batch when fennel is in season – eat half now and freeze the remaining half.

2 medium fennel bulbs (1kg)
40g butter
2 medium brown onions
   (300g), chopped coarsely
2 cloves garlic, quartered
2kg egg tomatoes, quartered
20g butter, extra
2 cloves garlic, crushed, extra
3 cups chicken or vegetable
   stock (750ml)

1 Trim fennel, discarding woody stalks and all but ½ cup of the fine uppermost leaves; reserve leaves. Chop about a third of the fennel finely; reserve. Chop remaining fennel coarsely.

2 Melt butter in large saucepan; cook coarsely chopped fennel, onion and garlic, stirring, until onion is soft. Add tomato; cook, uncovered, stirring occasionally, about 30 minutes or until tomato is very soft and pulpy.

3 Blend or process soup mixture, in batches, until smooth then pass through a food mill or fine sieve back into same pan.

4 Heat extra butter in small frying pan; cook extra garlic and finely chopped fennel, stirring, until fennel is just soft and golden brown. Add to soup with stock; bring to a boil. *[Can be made ahead to this stage. Cover; refrigerate overnight or freeze.]*

5 Simmer about 5 minutes or until soup is hot. Just before serving, stir in finely chopped reserved fennel leaves.

SERVES 6

per serve 8.9g fat; 799kJ
serving suggestion Great served as a prelude to a main course of lamb shank casserole.

tips If you prefer, substitute either a teaspoon of sour cream or Pernod to each bowl of soup in place of the fennel leaves.

• If you don't own a food mill (sometimes called a mouli) or prefer to use a handheld stab mixer, the tomatoes must be peeled.

How to peel tomatoes
Remove the woody core at the top of each tomato.
Cover tomatoes with boiling water in a heatproof bowl.
When skin wrinkles, peel away from the core to the base.
Using sharp knife, pull away and discard all the tomato skin.

white gazpacho

PREPARATION TIME 25 MINUTES (plus standing time)

An uncooked soup always served cold, white gazpacho reflects the Moorish influence on the food of the south of Spain; the use of ground almonds and freshly chopped herbs in a soup is more North African than Spanish. Almond meal (sometimes sold as ground almonds), as the name suggests, is a coarse flour made by pulverising almonds.

**6 slices white bread
(approximately 250g)**
2 tablespoons dry sherry vinegar
3 cups water (750ml)
1¹/2 cups almond meal (185g)
**2 tablespoons coarsely
chopped fresh chervil**
**2 Lebanese cucumbers (260g),
seeded, chopped finely**
1 teaspoon salt
1 cup cream (250ml)
**1¹/2 tablespoons extra virgin
olive oil**

1 Remove and discard crusts from bread; combine remaining bread in large non-reactive bowl with vinegar and the water; stand 15 minutes. Whisk in almond meal and half of the chervil.

2 Meanwhile place cucumber in colander; sprinkle with salt, stand 15 minutes. Rinse cucumber under cold water; drain on absorbent paper.

3 Blend or process bread mixture and cream, in batches, until pureed. Return soup mixture to same cleaned bowl; stir in cucumber. *[Can be made ahead to this stage. Cover; refrigerate overnight.]*

4 Divide soup among serving bowls; drizzle with oil, sprinkle with remaining chervil.

SERVES 6

per serve 30.4g fat; 1438kJ

serving suggestion Accompany with an array of tapas (the Spanish equivalent of antipasti) and fresh bread.

tip You can substitute fresh mint leaves for the chervil and red wine vinegar for the sherry vinegar.

Soaking bread in the vinegared water

corn and lemon grass soup with fish cakes

PREPARATION TIME 25 MINUTES • COOKING TIME 35 MINUTES

8 corn cobs (approximately 3.5kg)
1 tablespoon peanut oil
1 large brown onion (200g),
    chopped finely
2 cloves garlic, crushed
1 tablespoon grated fresh ginger
1/3 cup coarsely chopped
    fresh lemon grass
500g pumpkin, chopped coarsely
3 cups vegetable stock (750ml)
1.5 litres water (6 cups)

FISH CAKES
2 green onions,
    chopped coarsely
2 tablespoons coarsely chopped
    fresh coriander leaves
400g boneless firm white fish
    fillets, chopped coarsely
2 tablespoons torn fresh
    Vietnamese mint leaves
1 red Thai chilli, quartered
1 egg
4 kaffir lime leaves, torn
1 tablespoon sliced fresh ginger
2 cloves garlic, quartered
2 tablespoons peanut oil

1 Cut kernels from corn cobs; discard cobs.

2 Heat oil in large saucepan; cook onion, garlic, ginger and lemon grass, stirring, until onion softens. Add corn and pumpkin; cook, stirring, 5 minutes.

3 Add stock and the water, bring to a boil; simmer, covered, about 20 minutes or until pumpkin is tender.

4 Blend or process soup mixture, in batches, until pureed; push soup through food mill or large sieve into same cleaned pan; stir over heat until hot. *[Can be made ahead to this stage. Cover; refrigerate overnight or freeze.]* Serve soup with fish cakes.

fish cakes Process onion, coriander, fish, mint, chilli, egg, lime leaves, ginger and garlic until combined; using hands, roll level tablespoons of fish mixture into balls, shape balls into patty-shaped cakes (you will have

18 fish cakes). Place fish cakes on tray, cover; refrigerate 30 minutes. *[Can be made ahead to this stage. Cover; refrigerate overnight or freeze.]* Heat oil in large frying pan; cook fish cakes, in batches, until browned both sides and cooked through, drain on absorbent paper.

SERVES 6

per serve 15g fat; 1815kJ
serving suggestion Serve with a bowl of steamed jasmine rice.
tip Use kumara rather than pumpkin, if desired.

lamb and black-eye bean soup

PREPARATION TIME 35 MINUTES (plus standing time) • COOKING TIME 3 HOURS 40 MINUTES

Often called black-eyed peas, this small bone-coloured legume has a tiny black speck of an "eye" in the curve of one side. It is good in salads and on its own, as well as in meat stews and soups like this recipe.

Browning lamb shanks

Adding beans to soup

2 cups black-eye beans (400g)
2 medium red capsicums (400g)
1 tablespoon olive oil
1.5kg lamb shanks, trimmed
1 medium brown onion (150g),
  chopped coarsely
2 cloves garlic, quartered
2 medium carrots (240g),
  chopped coarsely
2 trimmed celery sticks (150g),
  chopped coarsely
2 tablespoons tomato paste
1 cup dry red wine (250ml)
3.5 litres water (14 cups)
1 tablespoon coarsely chopped
  fresh coriander leaves

1 Place beans in medium bowl, cover with water; soak overnight, drain.

2 Quarter capsicums, remove and discard seeds and membranes. Roast under grill or in very hot oven, skin-side up, until skin blisters and blackens. Cover capsicum pieces in plastic or paper for 5 minutes, peel away skin; chop finely.

3 Heat oil in large saucepan; cook lamb, in batches, until browned all over. Cook onion and garlic in same pan, stirring, until onion softens. Add carrot and celery; cook, stirring, 2 minutes. Add paste and wine, bring to a boil; simmer, uncovered, 5 minutes.

4 Add lamb and the water to pan; bring to a boil. Simmer, uncovered, 2 hours, skimming occasionally; strain through muslin-lined strainer into large bowl. Reserve lamb and stock; discard solids. *[Can be made ahead to this stage. Cover; refrigerate overnight or freeze.]*

5 When cool enough to handle, remove lamb meat from shanks; discard bones, shred lamb.

6 Return soup to same cleaned pan with beans, lamb and capsicum; stir over heat until hot. Just before serving soup, stir in coriander.

SERVES 6

per serve 12.5g fat; 1075kJ
serving suggestion Serve with warm crusty bread.

tip Turn the lamb so it browns all over, ensuring that the soup is as flavoursome as possible.

duck broth with rag pasta

PREPARATION TIME 30 MINUTES • COOKING TIME 2 HOURS

In Italy, "rag" pasta is usually the leftover scraps from homemade pasta dough; here, we've torn fresh lasagne sheets into irregular shapes. Ready-to-eat barbecued duck is available at specialist Chinese barbecued meat outlets as well as from some Chinese restaurants.

2 barbecued ducks (weighing approximately 1kg each)
1 tablespoon peanut oil
2 large brown onions (400g), chopped coarsely
5 star-anise
50g piece fresh ginger, sliced thinly
2 medium carrots (240g), chopped coarsely
2 trimmed celery sticks (150g), chopped coarsely
5 litres water (20 cups)
2 fresh lasagne sheets
100g tat soi, shredded finely
2 green onions, sliced thinly

1 Remove skin and meat from duck; reserve bones, discard skin, cut meat into thin pieces.

2 Heat oil in large saucepan; cook brown onion, star-anise and ginger, stirring, until onion softens. Add carrot and celery; cook, stirring, 2 minutes.

3 Add the water; bring to a boil, add reserved duck bones. Simmer, uncovered, 1¹/2 hours, skimming occasionally. Strain through muslin-lined strainer into large bowl. Reserve broth; discard solids. *[Can be made ahead to this stage. Cover; refrigerate overnight or freeze.]*

4 Tear pasta roughly into long strips.

5 Return duck broth to same cleaned pan with reserved duck meat and pasta; bring to a boil. Add pasta; simmer, uncovered, about 5 minutes or until pasta is just tender. Just before serving, stir in tat soi and green onion.

SERVES 6

per serve 11.3g fat; 1471kJ

serving suggestion Accompany with steamed rice and stir-fried bok choy with ginger and garlic.

tips Chicken can be substituted for duck, and pappardelle or egg noodles for lasagne.

Finely shredding tat soi

• Dust any excess flour from pasta to prevent the broth from becoming cloudy.

• Prepare stock the day before required; discard any solidified fat from surface before reheating.

leek soup with parmesan potato dumplings

PREPARATION TIME 30 MINUTES • COOKING TIME 55 MINUTES

50g butter
1 medium brown onion (150g),
chopped coarsely
2 cloves garlic, quartered
3 large leeks (1.5kg),
sliced thinly
2 large potatoes (600g),
chopped coarsely
3 cups vegetable stock (750ml)
1.5 litres water (6 cups)
^{1}/$_2$ cup cream (125ml)
1 tablespoon finely chopped
fresh garlic chives

PARMESAN POTATO DUMPLINGS
2 medium potatoes (400g),
chopped coarsely
20g butter
2 tablespoons sour cream
^{1}/$_4$ cup finely grated parmesan
cheese (20g)
2 tablespoons finely chopped
fresh garlic chives
1 cup self-raising flour (150g)
1 egg, beaten lightly

1 Melt butter in large saucepan; cook onion, garlic and leek, stirring, until leek softens.

2 Add potato, stock and the water, bring to a boil; simmer, covered, 25 minutes.

3 Blend or process soup mixture, in batches, until smooth. *[Can be made ahead to this stage. Cover; refrigerate overnight or freeze.]*

4 Return soup to same cleaned pan; stir over heat until hot. Drop rounded tablespoons of dumpling mixture into soup; simmer, uncovered, about 10 minutes or until dumplings are cooked through, stirring occasionally to turn dumplings. Stir in cream and chives.

parmesan potato dumplings
Boil, steam or microwave potato until tender; drain. Mash potato, butter and sour cream in medium bowl until smooth; add remaining ingredients, mix well.

SERVES 6

per serve 24.3g fat; 1976kJ
serving suggestion Rye bread is an excellent accompaniment.

Dropping dumplings into hot soup

seafood soup with gremolata

PREPARATION TIME 30 MINUTES • COOKING TIME 1 HOUR 20 MINUTES

Gremolata is the traditional Italian fresh accompaniment to osso buco, but it also partners other tomato-based dishes well.

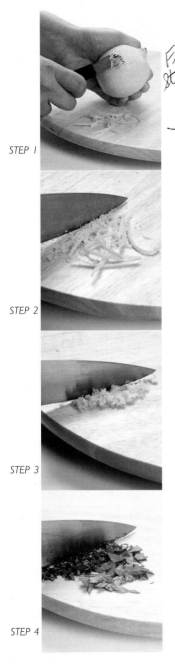

STEP 1

STEP 2

STEP 3

STEP 4

2kg fish bones
1 medium brown onion (150g),
  chopped coarsely
1 medium carrot (120g),
  chopped coarsely
2 trimmed celery sticks (150g),
  chopped coarsely
4 litres water (16 cups)
8 black peppercorns
2 bay leaves
1 tablespoon olive oil
1 medium brown onion (150g),
  chopped coarsely, extra
2 cloves garlic, crushed
5 medium tomatoes
  (950g), chopped
3 teaspoons sugar
400g can tomatoes
1/4 cup tomato paste (60g)
1/2 cup dry white wine (125ml)
2 medium uncooked
  lobster tails (760g),
  shelled, chopped coarsely
400g boneless firm white fish
  fillets, chopped coarsely

GREMOLATA

1 clove garlic, chopped finely
1 tablespoon finely chopped
  lemon rind
2 tablespoons finely chopped
  fresh flat-leaf parsley

handwritten: Fish stock

1 Combine fish bones, onion, carrot, celery, the water, peppercorns and bay leaves in large saucepan. Simmer, uncovered, 20 minutes. Strain stock over large bowl; discard bones and vegetables. *[Can be made ahead to this stage. Cover; refrigerate overnight or freeze.]*

2 Heat oil in large saucepan; cook extra onion and garlic, stirring, until onion softens. Add tomato and sugar; cook, stirring, about 10 minutes or until tomato is soft. Stir in undrained crushed tomatoes, paste and wine, bring to a boil; simmer, uncovered, about 5 minutes or until mixture has thickened slightly, stirring occasionally. Add stock, bring to a boil; simmer, uncovered, 20 minutes. Cool 10 minutes.

3 Blend or process tomato mixture, in batches, until pureed; return to same cleaned pan, bring to a boil. Add lobster and fish; simmer, stirring, about 5 minutes or until seafood is just cooked.

4 Divide soup among serving bowls; sprinkle each with gremolata.

gremolata Combine ingredients in small bowl.

SERVES 6

per serve 6.6g fat; 1232kJ
serving suggestion This soup is delicious with just a crisp baguette and a mesclun salad.

tip If you prefer, use prawns, crabs or yabbies instead of lobster.

Making gremolata
Use a zester to remove the lemon rind, avoiding the bitter white pith.
Cut the zested yellow rind shavings into the finest possible mince.
Finely mince the peeled garlic clove, using a very sharp knife.
Remove parsley leaves from stems; chop leaves, combine ingredients.

watercress and lemon soup

PREPARATION TIME 20 MINUTES • COOKING TIME 20 MINUTES

Removing leaves from watercress stems

40g butter
1 medium brown onion (150g),
   chopped coarsely
2 cloves garlic, quartered
1/4 cup plain flour (35g)
2 litres chicken stock (8 cups)
400g watercress leaves
   (850g bunch approximately)
1/4 cup lemon juice (60ml)
1/4 cup sour cream (60ml)

1 Melt butter in large saucepan; cook onion and garlic, stirring,
   until onion softens.

2 Add flour; cook, stirring, until mixture bubbles and thickens.
   Gradually stir in stock; cook, stirring, until mixture boils and thickens.
   Add watercress and juice. Bring soup mixture to a boil; simmer,
   uncovered, 2 minutes.

3 Blend soup mixture, in batches, until smooth. *[Can be made ahead
   to this stage. Cover; refrigerate overnight or freeze.]*

4 Return soup to same cleaned pan, add sour cream; stir over
   heat until hot.

SERVES 6

per serve 10.3g fat; 838kJ

serving suggestion Serve with plain chicken sandwiches for a light lunch.

tip Crème fraîche can be substituted for the sour cream.

water spinach and beef soup

PREPARATION TIME 20 MINUTES (plus marinating time)
COOKING TIME 10 MINUTES

Chinese water spinach is a mild, versatile vegetable with crunchy white stalks and tender, dark green leaves. It resembles a bunch of spinach (which can be substituted) but has longer, more flexible leaves.

500g beef fillet, sliced thinly
2 cloves garlic, crushed
3 green onions, sliced thinly
2 teaspoons fish sauce
1 teaspoon sugar
1 red Thai chilli, seeded, chopped finely
2 teaspoons grated fresh galangal
500g Chinese water spinach
1.5 litres water (6 cups)
2 tablespoons lemon juice
1/4 cup loosely packed torn fresh Vietnamese mint leaves

1 Place beef, garlic, onion, sauce, sugar, chilli and galangal in large bowl; toss to combine. Cover; refrigerate 3 hours or overnight.

2 Trim spinach stems; crush stems with meat mallet or rolling pin. Chop leaves coarsely.

3 Bring the water to a boil in large saucepan, add spinach and beef mixture; simmer, uncovered, 2 minutes.

4 Remove soup from heat; stir in remaining ingredients.

SERVES 6

per serve 3.6g fat; 525kJ
serving suggestion Serve with separate bowls of steamed jasmine rice.

tip This soup will be at its most flavoursome if you marinate the beef overnight and make the soup as close to serving time as possible.

GREEN PLATE FROM EMPIRE HOMEWARES

Crushing spinach stalks with rolling pin

Adding beef mixture to the pan

japanese noodle soup

PREPARATION TIME 20 MINUTES • COOKING TIME 15 MINUTES

There are restaurants all over Japan specialising in handmade soba (buckwheat noodle) soups, popular for their delicious flavour as much as for their restorative qualities. The Japanese ingredients called for here are available in Asian food stores and in most large supermarkets. Make this soup as close to serving time as possible.

300g fresh firm tofu
1 medium carrot (120g)
2 green onions
1/3 cup brown miso (80g)
2.5 litres water (10 cups)
3 teaspoons dashi granules
1 1/2 teaspoons wasabi
1 tablespoon tamari
200g soba
1 sheet toasted nori, shredded
2 teaspoons finely chopped pickled ginger

Finely chopping pickled ginger

1 Cut tofu into 1cm cubes.

2 Using vegetable peeler, peel carrot into ribbons; cut ribbons into thin strips. Cut onions into similar-length thin strips.

3 In small bowl, combine miso with 1 cup of the water. Combine remaining water, dashi, wasabi and tamari in large saucepan; bring to a boil. Add soba and half of the nori; boil, stirring with a fork, until soba is just tender.

4 Remove pan from heat; stir in miso mixture, tofu, carrot and onion. Serve immediately, topped with remaining nori and ginger.

SERVES 6

per serve 7.3g fat; 1308kJ

serving suggestion Accompany this soup with a tempura platter.

tips Regular soy sauce can be substituted for tamari, and fresh grated ginger can be substituted for pickled ginger.

• Stir a little leftover wasabi into a cup of homemade mayonnaise or aioli, and eat with crudités as a snack.

rocket and pancetta soup

PREPARATION TIME 20 MINUTES • COOKING TIME 35 MINUTES

Placing pancetta in single layer on oven tray

This soup should be made just before serving.

100g thinly sliced pancetta
1 tablespoon olive oil
1 medium red onion (170g),
 chopped coarsely
2 cloves garlic, quartered
1¹/₂ tablespoons balsamic vinegar
4 medium potatoes (800g),
 chopped coarsely
3 cups chicken stock (750ml)
3 cups water (750ml)
500g rocket, trimmed
¹/₄ cup finely grated parmesan
 cheese (20g)

1 Preheat oven to moderate.

2 Place pancetta in single layer on oven tray; roast, uncovered, in moderate oven, about 15 minutes or until crisp. Drain pancetta on absorbent paper then chop coarsely.

3 Heat oil in large saucepan; cook onion and garlic, stirring, until onion softens. Add vinegar and potato; cook, stirring, 5 minutes.

4 Add stock and the water; bring to a boil. Simmer, uncovered, about 15 minutes or until potato softens. Stir in rocket; cook, stirring, about 2 minutes or until rocket is wilted.

5 Blend or process soup mixture, in batches, until smooth. Return soup to same cleaned pan, stir over heat until hot. Divide soup among serving bowls; sprinkle each with cheese and pancetta.

SERVES 6

per serve 7g fat; 855kJ
serving suggestion Serve with tomato and basil bruschetta.
tip Prosciutto can be substituted for pancetta.

pumpkin risotto soup

Arborio rice is a short, round grain having a high starch content. Pepato cheese is a tangy pecorino-romano studded with black peppercorns. If you prefer, substitute it with plain romano or parmesan and a hefty dose of freshly ground black pepper.

1kg pumpkin, chopped coarsely
1/4 cup olive oil (60ml)
1 medium leek (350g),
    sliced thinly
2 cloves garlic, quartered
1 cup arborio rice (200g)
1/2 cup dry white wine (125ml)
1.5 litres chicken stock (6 cups)
1 litre water (4 cups)
1/2 cup cream (125ml)
1/2 cup coarsely grated
    pepato cheese (40g)

1 Preheat oven to moderate.

2 Combine pumpkin and 1 tablespoon of the oil in large baking dish; bake in moderate oven, uncovered, about 25 minutes or until pumpkin browns and softens.

3 Heat remaining oil in large saucepan; cook leek and garlic, stirring, about 10 minutes or until leek is soft. Add rice; cook, stirring, 2 minutes. Add wine, bring to a boil; simmer, uncovered, 5 minutes.

4 Add stock and the water, bring to a boil; simmer, uncovered, about 20 minutes or until rice is tender. Cool 10 minutes then stir in pumpkin.

5 Blend or process half of the soup mixture, in batches, until smooth.

6 Return pureed soup to same pan with remaining unprocessed soup mixture, cream and half of the cheese; stir over heat until hot. Divide soup among serving bowls; sprinkle each with remaining cheese.

SERVES 6

per serve 18.3g fat; 1707kJ
serving suggestion Serve with soft white bread rolls and a baby spinach leaf salad.

tips Pepato isn't a particularly hard cheese so it can be crumbled as easily as grated.

• This soup should be made just before serving.

Coarsely grating pepato cheese

italian meatball soup

PREPARATION TIME 30 MINUTES • COOKING TIME 30 MINUTES

STEP 1

STEP 2

STEP 3

STEP 4

1 tablespoon olive oil
2 medium brown onions (300g), chopped coarsely
3 cloves garlic, quartered
10 medium tomatoes (approximately 2kg), chopped coarsely
3 cups vegetable stock (750ml)
4 red Thai chillies, seeded, chopped finely
2 tablespoons tomato paste
250g fusilli pasta
8 fresh basil leaves, shredded finely

MEATBALLS

500g minced beef
2 teaspoons finely chopped fresh oregano

1 Heat oil in large saucepan; cook onion and garlic, stirring, until onion softens.

2 Add tomato, stock, chilli and paste; bring to a boil. Simmer, uncovered, stirring occasionally, about 15 minutes or until tomato is pulpy.

3 Blend or process tomato mixture, in batches, until pureed; push through food mill or large sieve into same cleaned pan. *[Can be made ahead to this stage. Cover; refrigerate overnight or freeze.]*

4 Return soup to heat; bring to a boil. Add meatballs; simmer, uncovered, about 10 minutes or until meatballs are cooked through.

5 Meanwhile, cook pasta in large saucepan of boiling water, uncovered, until just tender; drain.

6 Just before serving soup, stir in pasta and basil.

meatballs Using hands, combine beef and oregano in large bowl; roll level tablespoons of mixture into balls. Place meatballs on tray, cover; refrigerate 30 minutes. *[Can be made ahead to this stage. Cover; refrigerate overnight or freeze.]*

SERVES 6

per serve 7.4g fat; 1476kJ

serving suggestion Accompany this soup with homemade potato and rosemary focaccia.

tips Do not seed the chillies if you prefer a spicier soup.

• Passing the soup through a food mill (sometimes called a mouli) will result in a velvety smooth texture.

• You can use any short pasta in place of the fusilli – try farfalle or penne.

A chiffonade of basil
Wash the basil then carefully remove eight of the largest leaves from stems.
Stack the leaves on top of one another; grip firmly and roll into tight cigar shape.
Using a sharp knife, cut across the "cigar" into the thinnest possible slices.
Unravel the finely sliced whorls of basil with your fingers: this is a chiffonade.

white bean soup with polenta croutons

PREPARATION TIME 20 MINUTES (plus refrigeration time)
COOKING TIME 35 MINUTES

1 tablespoon olive oil
2 small leeks (400g), sliced
2 cloves garlic, crushed
2 trimmed celery sticks
**   (150g), chopped**
1.5 litres chicken stock (6 cups)
1 tablespoon white
**   wine vinegar**
4 x 400g cans cannellini beans,
**   drained, rinsed**
1/2 cup cream (125ml)
2 teaspoons fresh thyme leaves

POLENTA CROUTONS

2 cups water (500ml)
1/2 cup polenta (85g)
1/4 cup finely grated parmesan
**   cheese (20g)**
1 red Thai chilli, seeded,
**   chopped finely**

1 Heat oil in large saucepan; cook leek and garlic, stirring, about 10 minutes or until leek is soft. Add celery; cook, stirring, 2 minutes.

2 Stir in stock, vinegar and 2 cans of the beans. Bring to a boil; simmer, covered, 10 minutes.

3 Blend or process bean mixture, in batches, until smooth. *[Can be made ahead to this stage. Cover; refrigerate overnight.]*

4 Combine bean mixture with remaining 2 cans of the beans, cream and thyme in same cleaned pan; stir over heat until soup is hot.

5 Just before serving, ladle soup into serving bowls; top with polenta croutons.

polenta croutons Grease 8cm x 26cm bar pan, line base and sides with baking paper. Place the water in medium saucepan, bring to a boil, gradually stir in polenta; cook, stirring, over low heat about 5 minutes or until mixture is thick, stir in cheese and chilli. Spread polenta in prepared pan. Cover; refrigerate 3 hours or overnight. Turn polenta out onto board; cut into 5mm slices, halve each slice. Heat oiled grill pan; cook polenta pieces, in batches, until brown all over. Drain on absorbent paper.

SERVES 6

per serve 18.1g fat; 1614kJ

tip Dried cannellini beans can be substituted for canned cannellini beans. Place 3 cups dried beans in medium bowl; cover with cold water, stand overnight, drain. Add beans, stock and vinegar to celery mixture, bring to a boil; simmer, covered, about 1 hour or until beans are tender.

GREEN PLATE AND BOWL FROM GRACE BROS

Cooking polenta until thick

chicken wonton soup

PREPARATION TIME 30 MINUTES • COOKING TIME 1 HOUR 45 MINUTES

You can buy bags of uncooked chicken bones at most poultry shops; you can also use chicken wings or necks if you like.

2kg chicken bones
2 medium carrots (240g), chopped coarsely
2 trimmed celery sticks (150g), chopped coarsely
2 medium brown onions (300g), chopped coarsely
50g piece ginger, sliced thinly
5 litres water (20 cups)
¼ cup soy sauce (60ml)
250g choy sum, trimmed, chopped coarsely
1 cup bean sprouts (80g)
2 tablespoons coarsely chopped fresh Vietnamese mint leaves
4 green onions, sliced thinly

CHICKEN WONTONS

170g chicken breast fillet, chopped coarsely
1 small brown onion (150g), chopped coarsely
2 tablespoons coarsely chopped fresh Vietnamese mint leaves
36 wonton wrappers
1 egg, beaten lightly

1 Combine bones, carrot, celery, brown onion, ginger and the water in large saucepan; bring to a boil. Simmer, uncovered, 2 hours; strain through muslin-lined strainer into large bowl. Reserve stock; discard bones and vegetables. *[Can be made ahead to this stage. Cover; refrigerate overnight or freeze.]*

2 Return stock to same cleaned pan with soy sauce; bring to a boil. Add chicken wontons; simmer, uncovered, about 10 minutes or until wontons float to surface.

3 Just before serving soup, stir in remaining ingredients.

chicken wontons Blend or process chicken, onion and mint until almost smooth. Brush edge of each wonton wrapper with egg, place level teaspoon of chicken mixture in centre, pinch edge together to seal; repeat with remaining wrappers and chicken mixture.

SERVES 6

per serve 2.1g fat; 832kJ

serving suggestion Accompany with a side dish of finely chopped red Thai chillies, extra soy sauce and chopped mint.

tips Make the stock the day before required; refrigerate stock overnight, covered. Lift solidified fat from surface of stock; discard.

• Baby corn, bamboo shoots and other small, trimmed vegetables can be added to this soup.

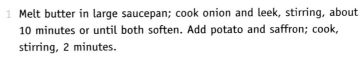

oyster and saffron soup

PREPARATION TIME 20 MINUTES • COOKING TIME 45 MINUTES

80g butter
1 large brown onion (200g), chopped coarsely
1 medium leek (350g), chopped coarsely
4 medium potatoes (800g), chopped coarsely
6 saffron threads
1.5 litres fish stock (6 cups)
1 litre water (4 cups)
24 oysters, shelled
1/2 cup cream (125ml)
2 tablespoons lemon juice
1/4 cup finely chopped fresh chives

Removing oysters from shells

1 Melt butter in large saucepan; cook onion and leek, stirring, about 10 minutes or until both soften. Add potato and saffron; cook, stirring, 2 minutes.

2 Add stock and the water; bring to a boil. Simmer, uncovered, about 15 minutes or until potato softens. Remove from heat, add half of the oysters; cool 10 minutes.

3 Blend or process soup mixture, in batches, until smooth. *[Can be made ahead to this stage. Cover; refrigerate overnight.]*

4 Return soup to same cleaned pan with remaining oysters, cream and juice; stir over heat until hot. Just before serving soup, stir in chives.

SERVES 6

per serve 21.2g fat; 1341kJ

serving suggestion Oyster and saffron soup is great for a special occasion or holiday, like Christmas dinner.

tip You can substitute 1/2 teaspoon ground turmeric for the saffron to achieve the right colour.

asparagus soup with polenta dumplings

PREPARATION TIME 25 MINUTES • COOKING TIME 55 MINUTES

1 Melt butter in large saucepan; cook onion and leek, stirring, about 10 minutes or until both are soft.

2 Add flour; cook, stirring, until mixture bubbles and thickens. Gradually add stock; cook, stirring, until mixture boils and thickens. Add asparagus, bring to a boil; simmer, uncovered, stirring occasionally, 30 minutes.

3 Blend or process soup mixture, in batches, until smooth. *[Can be made ahead to this stage. Cover; refrigerate overnight or freeze.]*

4 Return soup to same cleaned pan; bring to a boil. Drop level tablespoons of dumpling mixture into soup; cook, uncovered, stirring occasionally, about 15 minutes or until dumplings are cooked through. Just before serving soup, stir in pepper.

polenta dumplings Bring the water to a boil in medium saucepan. Gradually stir in polenta; cook, stirring, about 5 minutes or until mixture thickens. Add remaining ingredients; mix well. Dumpling mixture will be soft and sticky.

SERVES 6

per serve 19g fat; 1898kJ

serving suggestion This soup is perfect served with a tomato and bocconcini salad.

100g butter
1 medium brown onion (150g), chopped coarsely
1 medium leek (350g), chopped finely
1/2 cup plain flour (75g)
2 litres chicken stock (8 cups)
750g fresh asparagus, trimmed, chopped
1 teaspoon cracked black pepper

POLENTA DUMPLINGS
2 cups water (500ml)
1 cup polenta (170g)
3/4 cup coarsely grated parmesan cheese (60g)
1/2 cup self-raising flour (75g)
1/4 cup milk (60ml)

celeriac and walnut soup

PREPARATION TIME 20 MINUTES • COOKING TIME 35 MINUTES

Coarsely chopping toasted walnuts

Pushing soup mixture through a food mill

1 tablespoon olive oil

**1 medium brown onion (150g),
    chopped coarsely**

2 cloves garlic, quartered

**2 medium celeriac
    (approximately 850g trimmed,
    peeled), chopped coarsely**

**3 trimmed celery sticks (225g),
    chopped coarsely**

**2 medium carrots (240g),
    chopped coarsely**

1.5 litres vegetable stock (6 cups)

1 litre water (4 cups)

2 bay leaves

**1¹/₂ cups walnut pieces (150g),
    toasted, chopped coarsely**

1 Heat oil in large saucepan; cook onion and garlic, stirring, until onion softens. Add celeriac; cook, stirring, 5 minutes. Add celery and carrot; cook, stirring, 5 minutes.

2 Add stock, the water and bay leaves, bring to a boil; simmer, covered, about 1 hour or until celeriac is soft.

3 Reserve ¹/₄ cup walnuts; stir remainder into soup mixture.

4 Blend or process soup mixture, in batches, until pureed; push through food mill or large sieve into same cleaned pan.

5 Return soup to heat; stir over heat until soup is hot. Divide soup among serving bowls; sprinkle each with remaining walnuts.

SERVES 6

per serve 21.1g fat; 1240kJ

serving suggestion Serve with linseed or wholegrain crackers.

tip Don't peel the celeriac until you're ready to cook it; the flesh turns brown when exposed to air.

making good soups great

Since Neolithic times, soup has been known to possess restorative and nourishing qualities – the aged and infirm were kept alive by being fed simple meat broths. This concept may have developed over the aeons, but the premise remains the same: each of us can remember our mother perched on the edge of our sickbed, holding a bowl of chicken broth and urging us to eat because "it'll make you feel better".

Soup can be quickly made from a few inexpensive ingredients, and recent studies show that prefacing a meal with a low-fat soup can help with weight loss by decreasing appetite for the following courses.

Soups form a staple food group in any cuisine, and are all improved if based on homemade stock (see recipes on pages 4 to 5). But the convenience, ease and speed of preparation afforded by the use of packaged stocks and demi-glaces, stock cubes and powder can't be denied. Use the best-quality prepared stock bases you can find, but bear in mind that prepared stock bases can be very salty and/or full of kilojoules.

homemade stock tips

Any of our basic stock recipes (pages 4 to 5) can take on Mediterranean or Asian undertones with a bit of ingenuity. Add fresh herbs shortly before the stock is finished, and dry-fry spices separately, until they are just fragrant, before adding to the basic stock ingredients at the start of preparation.

■ Chopped chilli, fish sauce, kaffir lime leaves and lemon grass impart the taste of Thai seasonings.

■ Torn fresh oregano or basil leaves and crushed garlic cloves convert stock into an Italian soup base (try adding a tablespoon of pesto as an alternative).

■ Cumin, preserved lemon, cinnamon and a teaspoon of harissa are redolent of Moroccan dishes.

■ Add lots of chopped parsley, and some olive oil, lemon juice and a dash of allspice to bring the taste of Lebanon to your stockpot.

Other tips for homemade stock include:

■ Clarify stock by stirring 1 lightly beaten egg white and 1 cracked eggshell per litre of stock into a pot of fairly cool stock. Return pot to low heat; slowly return stock to a simmer, without stirring. Simmer 15 minutes, ignoring frothy scum that appears on surface of stock. Take stockpot off heat; cool for about 30 minutes. Using a ladle, push scum aside; scoop stock into muslin-lined sieve placed over a large bowl. Refrigerate until you're ready to freeze or use the stock.

■ Before freezing stock, you should refrigerate it until cold. Any grease in stock rises to form a solid surface; carefully scoop this fat off the top of stock and either discard it or, if you're frying another dish for the same meal, consider using it as the frying medium.

■ If you want to use stock straightaway and have no time to congeal the grease, try blotting the surface of soup gently with a few sheets of absorbent paper.

■ Freeze this degreased cooled stock in quantities to suit your needs. It can be frozen in empty, cleaned 300ml, 600ml or 1 litre milk cartons; fill to about 3cm from the top of container, cover with a small plastic bag and stand upright in the freezer until frozen. Stock expands as it freezes, so the gap left at the top and the looseness of the plastic bag allow for this. Once frozen solid, seal the stock in carton using masking tape or rubber bands, and stack cartons on their sides in freezer. You can also freeze stock in ice-cube trays; once frozen solid, place cubes in a snap-lock plastic bag and use singly or as required.

thickening soups

If you are heavy-handed with the stock, overzealous while pureeing or if you just like thick soup, try these thickening ideas.

■ First and most obvious is simply to simmer the soup, uncovered, until it cooks down to the desired thickness. Another simple idea is to puree some of the soup's solids (for instance, half of the beans or peas, or some of the potato and carrot) then return them to the pan to thicken the broth.

■ Spoon a little of the hot broth into a small bowl, cool it for 5 minutes, then whisk a few tablespoons of plain flour into it; once the flour mixture is smooth, stir it into the simmering soup.

■ Cornflour or arrowroot can also be blended with a little cold water; stir this mixture into simmering soup.

■ Grate a raw potato into the simmering pan of soup and stir until it is cooked and the liquid has thickened.

■ Beat a few of the egg yolks leftover from when you clarified the stock into a little of the hot broth in a separate small bowl, then whisk this mixture into the hot soup.

■ Cream, yogurt, sour cream, crème fraîche and even grated cheese can all be used to thicken those soups that will tolerate the addition of particular dairy products. It is advisable to stabilise the dairy product you're using by blending it with a little cornflour then whisking some of the hot stock into the cornflour mixture. Stir this mixture into your simmering soup.

serving containers and garnishes

■ A covered soup tureen and matching ladle make an especially spectacular way of presenting a main course soup at a special meal.

■ If you can, choose serving bowls to suit the soup (rice bowls for Oriental soups, small crocks for heavier European soups, and so on). If in doubt, probably the best container is a large flat soup bowl – they are easy to eat from and garnished soup looks fantastic within them.

Garnishes serve a practical, as well as aesthetic, purpose: shavings of pumpkin or carrot help identify orange-coloured soups; finely chopped chilli and coriander leaves turn a simple tomato broth into a Mexican delight; and sour cream and chopped chives are necessities for borscht.

Possibilities for appropriate garnishes can be:

■ *For thick soups:* slices of cucumber, lemon, onion or tomato; slices of toasted French bread with cheese melted over them; delicious dumplings; whole roasted tiny vegetables; or ravioli.

■ *For smooth or cream soups:* coarsely chopped or tiny whole leaves of herbs; contrasting coloured pureed vegetables or crème fraîche swirled into the surface; lightly fried shredded green onion or slices of garlic; or flavoured fried croutons.

■ *For broths or consommes:* finely shredded lemon zest; chiffonades of appropriate green herbs; a few crunchy fried noodles or tiny shards of toasted pitta or tortilla; hair-like strands of finely shredded carrot, cucumber, daikon or red onion.

tips for top soups

■ Don't overseason: when the soup is almost ready, test it for taste and, only then, add any necessary salt, pepper or other seasoning.

■ Buttermilk tastes great and is a lower-fat basis for a cream soup; likewise, pureed soup vegetables can replace a portion of the called-for amounts of cream or butter. Evaporated low-fat milk can also be used in part for some of the required cream.

■ Don't overcook or freeze soups that contain rice, pasta or potatoes; add these ingredients just before serving so that their texture remains slightly firm and resilient.

■ Defrost meat-based stocks in the refrigerator and always bring them to a boil before finishing the soup.

■ Some frozen soups need to be diluted and/or re-tasted for seasoning after they have thawed.

■ Small cubes of tofu can be stirred into almost-finished vegetable soups for added protein.

■ Various herbs and vegetables have particular qualities that they impart to soup, so it is best to consider them before using. For instance, celery leaves will cloud a stock; carrots will both darken and sweeten a broth; and the stalks of parsley, and some onions, can add a bitter flavour to stock.

glossary

RED LENTILS

PUY LENTILS

BLUE BOILERS

BROWN LENTILS

YELLOW LENTILS

almond meal also known as finely ground almonds; powdered to a flour-like texture, used in baking or as a thickening agent.

andouille a spicy smoked sausage used in gumbo, a mainstay of Louisiana's Creole cooking. Can be substituted with the more readily available chorizo.

bacon rashers also known as slices of bacon; made from pork side, cured and smoked. Streaky bacon is the fatty end of a bacon rasher (slice), without the lean (eye) meat.

beans
BLACK (TURTLE) Latin American and Caribbean small black bean with a tiny white eye, not to be confused with Chinese black (soy) beans. Available dried or canned.

BORLOTTI also known as Roman beans; pale pink with darker red spots, eaten fresh or dried.

CANNELLINI similar in appearance and flavour to other dried white beans such as great northern, navy and haricot; sold canned or dried, good in soups and casseroles.

KIDNEY medium-sized red bean, slightly floury yet sweet in flavour; sold dried or canned, used in soups, salads and stews.

beetroot also known as red beets or, simply, beets; firm, round deep purple-red root vegetable having a sweet distinctive taste and refined smooth texture. Can be eaten raw, grated in salads, boiled then sliced, or roasted then mashed like potatoes.

butter use salted or unsalted ("sweet") butter; 125g is equal to 1 stick butter.

buttermilk sold alongside all fresh milk products in supermarkets. A good lower-fat substitution for dairy products such as cream or sour cream; good in baking and in salad dressings.

capsicum also known as bell pepper or, simply, pepper. Seeds and membranes should be discarded before use.

cheese
BLUE mould-treated cheeses mottled with blue veining. Varieties include firm and crumbly Stilton types to mild, creamy brie-like cheeses.

PARMESAN a dry, hard cheese made from skim or part-skim milk and aged at least a year; the best are called grana or reggiano.

PEPATO sharp, tangy pecorino-romano studded with black peppercorns. Substitute with plain romano or parmesan and freshly ground black pepper.

ROMANO hard, straw-coloured cheese having a grainy texture and sharp, tangy flavour.

chervil also known as cicily; mildly fennel-flavoured herb with curly dark-green leaves.

chickpeas also called garbanzos, hummus or channa; an irregularly round, sandy-coloured legume.

chillies available in many types and sizes, both fresh and dried. Wear rubber gloves to seed and chop fresh chillies as they can burn your skin. Removing membranes and seeds lessens the heat level.

DUTCH a medium-hot, fairly long fresh chilli; also known as a Holland chilli.

GUAJILLO also called travieso or cascabel; the dried form of the fresh mirasol chilli. Deep-red to almost-black in colour, this medium-hot chilli must be soaked in boiling water before being used.

JALAPEÑO sold finely chopped or whole, bottled in vinegar, as well as fresh; we used the medium-hot, sweetish, chopped bottled version in our recipes.

SWEET CHILLI SAUCE comparatively mild, Thai-type sauce made from red chillies, sugar, garlic and vinegar.

THAI small, medium-hot, and bright-red to dark-green in colour.

chinese barbecued duck this duck has a sweet-sticky coating made from soy sauce, sherry, five-spice and hoisin sauce. It is available from Asian food stores.

chinese cooking wine made from rice, wheat, sugar and salt, with 13.5% alcohol; available from Asian food stores. Mirin or sherry can be substituted.

chinese green vegetables the same vegetables can be called by more than one name; we have listed many of the alternative names.

BOK CHOY also known as bak choy, pak choi, Chinese white cabbage, Chinese chard; has a mild, fresh mustard taste; use stems and leaves.

CHINESE SPINACH also known as amaranth, yin choy; sold with roots, which are pinkish red. Young shoots and leaves are the most tender.

CHOY SUM also known as flowering bok choy or flowering white cabbage.

WATER SPINACH also known as swamp spinach, long green, ung choy, kang kong.

chorizo a sausage of Spanish origin; made of coarsely ground pork and seasoned with garlic and chillies.

ciabatta Italian for slipper, which is the traditional shape of this popular crisp-crusted white bread.

coriander also known as cilantro or Chinese parsley; bright-green-leafed herb with a pungent flavour.

cornmeal ground dried corn (maize); similar to polenta but slightly coarser.

couscous a grain-like cereal product, originally from North Africa; made from semolina.

cream
CRÈME FRAÎCHE a mature fermented cream (minimum fat content 35%) having a slightly tangy flavour and velvety rich texture; similar thickness to sour cream.

FRESH also known as pure cream and pouring cream (minimum fat content 35%); has no additives like commercially thickened cream.

SOUR a thick, commercially cultured soured cream (minimum fat content 35%).

curry leaves available fresh or dried, having a mild curry flavour; use like bay leaves.

dashi Japanese prepared fish (bonito) stock, sold in liquid, powdered or granulated form.

eggplant also known as aubergine.

eggs some recipes call for raw or barely cooked eggs; exercise caution if there is a salmonella problem in your area.

flour, plain an all-purpose flour, made from wheat.

food mill also called a mouli; a rotary sieve used for liquidising and pureeing.

galangal also known as laos; a dried root that is a member of the ginger family, used whole or ground, having a piquant peppery flavour.

PEPATO CHEESE

VIETNAMESE MINT

garam masala a blend of spices, originating in North India, based on cardamom, cinnamon, cloves, coriander, fennel and cumin, roasted and ground together.

gravy beef boneless stewing beef which, slow-cooked, imbues stocks and casseroles with a subtle meat flavour.

green peppercorns soft, unripe berry of the pepper plant usually sold in brine. Has distinctive fresh taste.

hoisin sauce a thick, sweet and spicy Chinese paste made from salted fermented soy beans, onions and garlic.

jerusalem artichoke crunchy tuber that tastes a bit like a fresh water chestnut.

kale member of the cabbage family resembling a loose-leaved dark-green flower.

kalonji also called black onion seeds or nigella; astringent-tasting seed used in curries and sprinkled on home-made Arab breads such as pide and pitta.

LINGUIÇA

FRESH CHORIZO

ketjap manis Indonesian thick soy sauce which has sugar and spices added.

kaffir limes and leaves wrinkly-skinned, green fruit and its leaves from a small citrus tree originally grown in South Africa.

kitchen string use string made from a natural material specifically for use in cooking; a synthetic string will melt.

kumara Polynesian name of orange-fleshed sweet potato often confused with yam.

lemon grass a tall, clumping, lemon-smelling and -tasting, sharp-edged grass; the white lower part of the stem is used, finely chopped, in cooking.

lemon pepper seasoning a blend of crushed black pepper, lemon, herbs and spices.

linguiça a garlic-laden Portuguese sausage used in the classic soups of that country; substitute chorizo or any spicy dried sausage.

madeira a fortified wine; types range from gold and dry to rich, sweet and dark.

mince meat also known as ground meat.

mirin sweet, low-alcohol rice wine used in Japanese cooking; sometimes referred to simply as rice wine but not to be confused with sake, rice wine made for drinking.

noodles
BEAN THREAD VERMICELLI also known as bean thread noodles, or cellophane or glass noodles.

RICE STICK a dried noodle, available flat and wide or very thin; made from rice flour and water.

SOBA thin, long, pale-brown noodle made from buckwheat and plain flour.

SOMEN extremely thin dried wheat noodle from Japan; sometimes made with egg and called tamago somen.

UDON available fresh and dried; Japanese broad white wheat noodle.

nori sheets of paper-thin dried black seaweed.

okra also known as bamia or lady fingers; a green, ridged, oblong pod with a furry skin. Used to thicken stews and soups as well as impart flavour.

pancetta an Italian salt-cured pork roll, usually cut from belly pork; used chopped in many dishes to add flavour. Bacon can be substituted.

pasta
DITALI, DITALINI tiny, very short tubes of macaroni, often used in minestrone.

FARFALLE bow-tie shaped short pasta.

FRESH LASAGNE sold in the refrigerated section of supermarkets; suitable for making ravioli, tortellini, etc.

RISONI small rice-shaped pasta. Very similar to another small pasta, orzo; usually used as the pasta in soups.

TAGLIATELLE long, flat strips of pasta.

pide also known as Turkish bread; long flat loaves, or individual rounds, made from wheat flour and sprinkled with sesame or black onion seeds.

pitta also known as Lebanese bread; also spelled pita, this wheat-flour pocket bread is sold in large, flat pieces that separate into two thin rounds. Also available in small thick pieces called pocket pitta.

polenta a flour-like cereal made of ground corn (maize). Also the name of the dish made from it.

prawns also known as shrimp.

pulses
BLUE BOILERS variety of blue-green pea grown specifically for drying; once dried, they are split along a natural seam. Whole and split boilers are available in supermarkets and health-food stores.

LENTILS (RED, BROWN, YELLOW) dried pulses often identified by and named after their colour; also known as dhal.

PUY LENTILS fine, blue-green, fast-cooking lentil originally from Le Puy in France.

pumpkin also known as squash; we prefer to use butternut pumpkin.

rice
ARBORIO small, round-grained white rice that absorbs a large amount of cooking liquid.

CALROSE medium-size grain; can be used instead of either long- or short-grain varieties.

rocket also known as arugula, rugula and rucola. Peppery-tasting green leaf; eat raw in salads or cooked in soups, risottos and the like.

shrimp paste also known as trasi or blanchan; pungent, preserved, almost solid paste made of salted dried shrimp.

Sichuan pepper also known as Chinese pepper; small, red-brown aromatic seeds resembling peppercorns. They have a peppery-lemon flavour.

spinach correct name for the leafy green vegetable often called English spinach or, incorrectly, silverbeet.

star anise dried star-shaped pod; seeds taste of aniseed.

sukiyaki sauce bottled Japanese sauce; a blend of soy sauce, mirin, sugar and salt.

tahini rich, thick, sesame-seed paste.

tofu also known as bean curd; made similarly to cheese, from soy bean "milk". It is available fresh or vacuum-packed from supermarkets and Asian food stores. Fried tofu, small cubes of firm tofu already deep-fried, can be purchased ready for use.

vietnamese mint narrow-leafed pungent herb, also known as laksa leaf (daun laksa) and Cambodian mint.

vinegar
BALSAMIC authentic only from Modena, Italy; made from a regional wine of white Trebbiano grapes.

CIDER made from fermented apple juice.

SHERRY natural vinegar aged in oak according to the traditional Spanish system.

wasabi green horseradish used to make a fiery sauce.

wine the adage is that you should never cook with wine you wouldn't drink; we used good-quality dry white and red wine in our recipes.

wonton wrappers gow gee, egg or spring roll pastry sheets can be substituted.

BORLOTTI BEANS

BLACK (TURTLE) BEANS

CANNELLINI BEANS

KIDNEY BEANS

index

facts and figures

Wherever you live, you'll be able to use our recipes with the help of these easy-to-follow conversions. While these conversions are approximate only, the difference between an exact and the approximate conversion of various liquid and dry measures is but minimal and will not affect your cooking results.

dry measures

metric	imperial
15g	1/2oz
30g	1oz
60g	2oz
90g	3oz
125g	4oz (1/4lb)
155g	5oz
185g	6oz
220g	7oz
250g	8oz (1/2lb)
280g	9oz
315g	10oz
345g	11oz
375g	12oz (3/4lb)
410g	13oz
440g	14oz
470g	15oz
500g	16oz (1lb)
750g	24oz (11/2lb)
1kg	32oz (2lb)

oven temperatures

These oven temperatures are only a guide. Always check the manufacturer's manual.

	C° (Celsius)	F° (Fahrenheit)	Gas Mark
Very slow	120	250	1
Slow	150	300	2
Moderately slow	160	325	3
Moderate	180 - 190	350 - 375	4
Moderately hot	200 - 210	400 - 425	5
Hot	220 - 230	450 - 475	6
Very hot	240 - 250	500 - 525	7

liquid measures

metric	imperial
30ml	1 fluid oz
60ml	2 fluid oz
100ml	3 fluid oz
125ml	4 fluid oz
150ml	5 fluid oz (1/4 pint/1 gill)
190ml	6 fluid oz
250ml	8 fluid oz
300ml	10 fluid oz (1/2 pint)
500ml	16 fluid oz
600ml	20 fluid oz (1 pint)
1000ml (1 litre)	13/4 pints

helpful measures

metric	imperial
3mm	1/8in
6mm	1/4in
1cm	1/2in
2cm	3/4in
2.5cm	1in
5cm	2in
6cm	21/2in
8cm	3in
10cm	4in
13cm	5in
15cm	6in
18cm	7in
20cm	8in
23cm	9in
25cm	10in
28cm	11in
30cm	12in (1ft)

helpful measures

The difference between one country's measuring cups and another's is, at most, within a 2 or 3 teaspoon variance. (For the record, 1 Australian metric measuring cup holds approximately 250ml.) The most accurate way of measuring dry ingredients is to weigh them. When measuring liquids, use a clear glass or plastic jug with the metric markings. (One Australian metric tablespoon holds 20ml; one Australian metric teaspoon holds 5ml.)

If you would like to purchase *The Australian Women's Weekly* Test Kitchen's metric measuring cups and spoons (as approved by Standards Australia), turn to page 120 for details and order coupon. You will receive:

■ a graduated set of 4 cups for measuring dry ingredients, with sizes marked on the cups.
■ a graduated set of 4 spoons for measuring dry and liquid ingredients, with amounts marked on the spoons.

Note: North America, NZ and the UK use 15ml tablespoons. All cup and spoon measurements are level.

We use large eggs having an average weight of 60g.

how to measure

When using graduated metric measuring cups, shake dry ingredients loosely into the appropriate cup. Do not tap the cup on a bench or tightly pack the ingredients unless directed to do so. Level top of measuring cups and measuring spoons with a knife. When measuring liquids, place a clear glass or plastic jug with metric markings on a flat surface to check accuracy at eye level.

Looking after your interest...

Keep your Home Library cookbooks clean, tidy and within easy reach with slipcovers designed to hold up to 12 books. *Plus* you can follow our recipes perfectly with a set of accurate measuring cups and spoons, as used by *The Australian Women's Weekly* Test Kitchen.

TO ORDER

Mail or fax Photocopy or complete the coupon below and post to AWW Home Library Reader Offer, ACP Direct, PO Box 7036, Sydney NSW 1028, *or* fax to (02) 9267 4363.

Credit cards Have your details ready then, if you live in Sydney, phone 9260 0000; if you live elsewhere in Australia, phone 1800 252 515 (free call, Mon-Fri, 8.30am-5.30pm).

PRICE

Book Holder
Australia: $13.15.
Elsewhere: $A21.95.

Metric Measuring Set
Australia: $6.55.
New Zealand: $A8.00.
Elsewhere: $A9.95.
Prices include postage, handling and GST.
This offer is available in all countries.

PAYMENT

Australian residents We accept the credit cards listed on the coupon, money orders and cheques.

Overseas residents We accept the credit cards listed on the coupon, drafts in $A drawn on an Australian bank, and also British, New Zealand and U.S. cheques in the currency of the country of issue. Credit card charges are at the exchange rate current at the time of payment.

- -

☐ **BOOK HOLDER**   ☐ **METRIC MEASURING SET**

Please indicate number(s) required.

Mr/Mrs/Ms _____

Address _____

_____

Postcode _____ Country _____

Ph: Bus. Hours:(   ) _____

I enclose my cheque/money order for $ _____ payable to ACP Direct

OR: please charge my

☐ Bankcard ☐ Visa ☐ MasterCard ☐ Diners Club ☐ Amex

Expiry Date ____/____

Cardholder's signature _____

Please allow up to 30 days for delivery within Australia. Allow up to 6 weeks for overseas deliveries. Both offers expire 31/01/01.
HLSOU00